JAMAICA OF TODAY

A banana carrier with a good load, Jamaica

JAMAICA OF TODAY

By

A. HYATT VERRILL

Author of *"West Indies of Today,"* **etc.**

Illustrated

DODD, MEAD AND COMPANY
NEW YORK   1931

PRINTED IN THE UNITED STATES OF AMERICA
BY THE VAIL-BALLOU PRESS, INC., BINGHAMTON, N. Y.

TABLE OF CONTENTS

[v]

TABLE OF CONTENTS

TABLE OF CONTENTS

TABLE OF CONTENTS

TABLE OF CONTENTS

[ix]

TABLE OF CONTENTS

ILLUSTRATIONS

[xi]

ILLUSTRATIONS

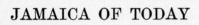

JAMAICA OF TODAY

Oh, some be for the lily,
An' some be for the rose,
But I be for the sugar cane
That in Jamaicy grows;
For 'tis that as makes the toddy
To warm me copper nose.

(Buccaneers' song)

THE first tourist to visit Jamaica was Columbus, and he did so from necessity rather than from choice. But he and his marooned sailors waxed as enthusiastic over the island's climate, beauty and possibilities as thousands since his time have been after visiting this largest of Britain's West Indian possessions. Yet it is only within comparatively recent years that Jamaica has become a popular winter resort for northern visitors, and even to-day it is not one tenth as popular as it should be. Why this should be so is something of a puzzle. Every year thousands—yes, tens of thousands—of people flock to tropical and semi-tropical lands. They cruise about the Caribbean and visit the historic spots along the Spanish Main; they idle away the days in Bermuda, swank in Florida or Nassau, swelter in Trinidad and indulge in a wild orgy of "whoopee" in Havana, and of course a portion of the multitudes find their way to Jamaica.

Yet not one of these more highly favored and more popular winter playgrounds can boast of the manifold attractions of Jamaica. Cuba is perhaps the most overrated of the West Indies. It—or rather I should say Havana—is not even tropical,

[1]

and during the winter often is so cold as to necessitate heavy woolen clothing and fur coats. It is one of the most expensive places on earth, it has very little of the foreign or exotic atmosphere remaining, and its greatest attractions are its opportunities for unlimited gambling. Nassau, beautiful as it is, is an expensive place and very limited in size and possibilities. No spot in Florida can be depended upon for continuous warm weather during the winter, and Florida possesses no scenery worthy of the name. As for the South and Central American cities, few tourists care to remain long in a Spanish-speaking land, unless they are familiar with the language, while hotel accommodations are none too good. And while the Lesser Antilles are among the most lovely and most delightful spots on earth, yet they have never yet really catered to visitors; the hotels are poor or worse and conditions are rather primitive.

Puerto Rico possesses lovely scenery, splendid motor roads, many excellent hotels, and is, of course, under the United States flag. But Puerto Rico does not hold much allure for more than a brief visit. In the first place it is as dry—theoretically—as the States themselves, and outside of San Juan and Ponce one must put up with many annoyances and inconveniences in the way of meals and sleeping accommodations. As for Santo

Courtesy of Duperly

Bournemouth Bath, Kingston, Jamaica, the finest sea-water bathing pool in the British West Indies

Courtesy of George Pearson, Kingston

Constant Spring Golf Club, near Kingston. H. R. H. the Prince of Wales, opened the new course at Constant Spring. It is the finest course in the West Indies

Domingo, filled as it is with historical associations and ancient buildings, magnificent as is its scenery, splendid as are its newly constructed highways, yet it is one of the last places where winter visitors would care to remain for long, unless they are of the type who enjoy roughing it, who crave the wilds and who scoff at luxuries and conveniences and all the amenities of our modern life.

Yet Jamaica possesses every advantage and none of the disadvantages of all—aside from gambling places and ancient Spanish buildings and remains. Its climate, especially in winter, is ideal, and if one is not satisfied with the climate in one spot it is only necessary to travel a few miles or a few thousand feet in order to find anything in the way of climate from the torrid to a very cool temperate zone. It has perhaps the most varied scenery in the West Indies—towering mountains, broad plains, rolling uplands, dark swamps, smiling valleys, deep cañons, high plateaus, grassy pastures, broad cultivated fields, rushing rivers, roaring cataracts, delectable sea beaches, charming coves, while everywhere is the rankest, most luxuriant tropical vegetation, the most gorgeous of tropic flowers and the most luscious of tropical fruits.

Its government is as solid, as stable and as dependable as that of England itself. Its laws are

[3]

just and liberal and do not discriminate against aliens. Its money does not fluctuate, and our own currency passes readily everywhere. The universal language is English. The natives are cheerful, willing, hospitable, orderly and law-abiding.

One can travel everywhere throughout the island by automobile or by railway. There is every form of recreation—hunting, fishing, polo, horse racing, tennis, golf, boating, etc. It is not an expensive place in which to live. It is one of the most healthful of tropical localities and it is clean and sanitary, with excellent water and an abundance of most delectable food, and it boasts some of the finest hotels anywhere in the tropics. Moreover, it is accessible from the United States, from Europe or from the other islands of the Caribbean. It is but one day's sail from Cuba, five days from New York. There are no venomous serpents and few noxious insects on the island; and finally the Jamaicans are anxious to welcome visitors and to make them feel at home, and they offer every courtesy and service to those who drop in to their charming island.

Possibly the fact that Kingston has been destroyed by an earthquake and that hurricanes have often devastated Jamaica has something to do with preventing northerners from flocking to the island as they do to Cuba and elsewhere. But hurricanes occur only during a few months in summer, and we must remember that Charleston and San Francisco both have been razed by quakes.

Largely, I think, the lack of wholesale invasions of winter visitors is due to the public's ignorance of Jamaica. Publicity—such propaganda as that of Cuba, the Bahamas, the Bermudas and Florida, which keeps those places constantly in the public mind and eye—has not been much in evidence regarding Jamaica. As a result, the average person thinks of Jamaica—when he thinks of it at all— as a terribly hot, a rather primitive place, associated with rum, bananas and ginger; and he pictures it as one vast banana grove, with a few acres of ginger and sugar cane, outside of which is dense jungle and swamps, the whole inhabited by lazy, filthy blacks.

Nothing could be further from the truth. Aside from the higher mountain sides, no jungle or primeval forest remains in Jamaica. Even on the coasts the temperature in winter is never excessive and is very equable, while in most places the trade wind—locally known "The Doctor"—blows constantly with refreshing coolness.

But to paint the true picture of Jamaica, to describe its attractions, its advantages, its scenery, its vegetation, its people and its allurements, in full detail, would require several volumes rather

[5]

than one. It is not my purpose to attempt this in the present work, but rather to give a brief sketch, an outline or horizon of Jamaica's manifold attractions, with enough of history, enough of geography and other information to give my readers an idea of what Jamaica has to offer, the whole seasoned with bits of interesting incidents and anecdotes, with strange fragments of the island's past. For the benefit of those who desire more concrete facts and definite data, such facts and figures will be found in condensed form, alphabetically arranged, thus forming a sort of abbreviated guide book quite apart from the rest of the volume.

In writing this book I have endeavored to deal with such features, such matters and such descriptions as will interest the average person. And if I appear to have devoted considerable space to such subjects as Jamaica's history and Jamaica's colored population, it is because both are of paramount importance, and because they are matters a knowledge of which is not easily acquired by a casual visitor to the island, whereas such a visitor cannot avoid learning of the island's scenic and other attractions at first hand, even in a few days.

The great trouble in writing of such an island as Jamaica is to stop. Pages, volumes might be filled with descriptions, with praise, with appreciations of Jamaica. But what is the use? No matter how much is written, it would all be summed up in the quaintly spelled words of a document entitled: "A Briefe Journall, or a succinct and true relation of the most Remarkable Passages observed in the Voyage undertaken bye Captain William Jackson to the West Indies or Continent of America. Anno Domini 1642," in which the writer of the "Briefe Journall" records his impressions of Jamaica as follows:

"Ye Temperature of ye Climent, and Salubritie of ye Ayre, may be very well deserned in ye good complection and long life of ye Inhabitants, who here attaine to greater age than those in many of ye neighbourynge islandes.

"It is likewise watered with pleausant Springs and fresh Rivers, and wanteth noe store of safe convenient Harbors for Ships, both on the South and North shores thereof. For briefe, it affords, or can produce, whatsoever, or most things, affected by man, either for pleasure or profitte."

CHAPTER I

OPALESCENT, like a vision rather than a reality, Jamaica hovers upon the horizon. But slowly, as the ship draws nearer, hills and valleys take form and substance until it looms sharp-cut against the blue tropic sky, its lofty peaks crowned with fleecy clouds, its wooded mountain sides and broad fields of golden cane, its emerald acres of banana walks and its opulent verdure forming as beautiful a picture as ever one may see. And as the approaching voyager gazes upon the lush valleys, the surf-washed beaches, the rugged sea-worn crags, the endless rows of palms and the majestic mountains of this largest of the British West Indies, the island appears like an earthly paradise.

But Jamaica's history is far from being that of a paradise. It has been far more reminiscent of hell, for it has been a story of debauchery, butchery, bloodshed and violence. Had it been afflicted with a curse, Jamaica could scarcely have suffered more from both God and man; and as the steamer passes the tip of the long sand-spit which is known

[8]

as the Palisados, and which forms a natural
breakwater for Kingston's harbor—and drops
anchor off the quarantine station, she floats above
the ruins of what once was famous as the wicked-
est city on earth. For beneath the waters at the
harbor mouth lie the remains of Port Royal, once
the metropolis of the buccaneers.

Close at hand the present Port Royal broils in
the sun upon the low sandy point with the lazy
waves lapping gently upon the beach and the
marine railway, with boats drawn up on shore,
with the British flag fluttering in the trade wind
above the barracks and the quarantine station—a
sleepy little town, yet filled with interest and inti-
mate associations with Jamaica's past. As one
wanders about, picking a way over the rough
cobbles of the lanes, or crosses the sun-baked
parade ground, it is difficult to believe that this
was once the most important of West Indian
ports, and the richest city in the New World, a
town whose name was associated with every
crime, vice and villainy of man's devising. Today
all that remains of the old Port Royal is ancient
Fort Charles with its moats and drawbridges, its
damp dungeons, its quaint corners and grass-
grown embrasures with the antique, ornate guns
looking seaward, little changed since that distant
time when Admiral Nelson was in command here.

Leading from a low-ceilinged, heavily timbered guard room, a flight of narrow steps leads upward to a paved platform known as "Nelson's Quarter Deck." Here the famous sea fighter paced to and fro, peering as if from a ship's deck at the shimmering horizon, in constant expectation of sighting the sails of the French fleet heading in from the sea to attack Port Royal. Very probably Nelson might never have become a famous hero had the French attacked Jamaica, for the garrison at Fort Charles was weak and its guns inadequate to cope with the heavy armament of the French. Or again, the future admiral might have won even earlier distinction by a gallant defense, for when he was in charge of Port Royal in 1779, he was a mere boy scarcely twenty-one years of age.

Here, too, Nelson very nearly died long ere he had made a name for himself, for in 1780 he returned to Port Royal close to death with dysentery contracted on the San Juan expedition. And here at Port Royal he was nursed back to health and strength by a black woman, known as Cuba Cornwallis, who took the future admiral into her own home in order to care for him.

Fastened into the coral pink walls of the old fort is a brass tablet commemorating Nelson's occupancy of the fort and bearing the inscription:

[10]

JAMAICA OF TODAY

In this place
Dwelt
HORATIO NELSON
You who tread his footprints
Remember his glory.

But Nelson was by no means the only famous man who trod the flagging of old Fort Charles. Within its walls Sir Henry Morgan and many a less notorious buccaneer have drunk to the health of the King of England and the damnation of the King of Spain; and, through centuries of storms and battles, cataclysms and hurricanes, its stout old walls and battlements have passed uninjured and have looked down on many a strange sight, on wickedness and sin, on wild pirate revels, on bestial orgies and indescribable crimes. Under the shelter of its guns, storm-beaten, shot-scarred buccaneer ships have anchored, deep laden with loot; and towering, wall-sided frigates have swung to their moorings. It passed unscathed through the awful earthquake of 1692 and saw the heaving earth and angry waves destroy thousands of lives and sweep the city into the depths of the sea. And when in 1907, Kingston was crumbled to dust in a few minutes, and more modern forts collapsed like pasteboard, the old pink fort at Port Royal sustained no damage other than a crack in one of its centuries-old walls.

What a tale the old fortress could tell if only it could speak! What a story of debauchery and tragedy: the story of Port Royal of olden times— the city of the buccaneers! Very different from the village of today was that old Port Royal, a noisy, bustling, crowded town of several thousand houses, of thousands of inhabitants, of shops and markets, gambling dens and reeking drinking places, of brothels and lurid vice; a city of immense warehouses filled to overflowing with goods from every quarter of the earth; a port with shipyards and a careenage where a dozen or more ships were always to be seen, where scores of high-pooped, heavily armed vessels rode at anchor off the shore. A town whose people were more familiar with the Jolly Roger, the burgees of Coxton, Davis, Morgan, Red Legs, Wooden Leg, Montbars, Swan, Sharp or other buccaneer chieftains, than with the ensign of Great Britain. The acknowledged headquarters of the freebooters and proud of it, for Jamaica depended upon the buccaneers for its prosperity and the port was their clearing house. Indeed, the very existence of Jamaica depended upon the corsairs, for they were at once her maintenance and her protection. To have a buccaneer stronghold at the entrance of the har-

[12]

bor was like having a hornets' nest in one's doorway, and no enemy ship was likely to molest the island as long as the buccaneers foregathered at Port Royal.

Here from far and wide they came, bringing their loot and treasure, their chests of doubloons and pieces of eight, their caskets of jewels, their cargoes of ingots of silver and gold, their altar pieces and church plate, their satins and velvets, silks and brocades, their casks of wines and brandy, their bales of tobacco and all their miscellaneous cargoes from scuttled ships, ravished galleons and sacked towns, until so filled with the pirates' riches was Port Royal that it was acknowledged the wealthiest of all ports.

And rivaling if not surpassing its richness was its wickedness—evil of which Port Royal was as proud as it was of its wealth, for its inhabitants brazenly and openly boasted that their city was the nearest thing to hell that human depravity could devise. Swaggering, red-handed scoundrels strutted through the cobbled streets boasting of their villainies, the atrocities they had committed, and spending the gold they had won by torture and murder. Everywhere the coarse oaths, the curses and maudlin shouts of buccaneers echoed from dives and hovels. Sin ruled supreme; murders were of such frequent occurrence they cre-

[13]

ated no comment, and the only law was what each man carried in scabbard or holster. Oftimes some besotted, drink-mad cut-throat would run amuck, slashing and shooting all he met, until himself was shot or cut down. Rival pirates would have disputes and settle them by sword or pistol duel in the streets; while, to afford a bit of diversion, hapless prisoners would be brought ashore and slowly roasted over fires in the market place, or spread-eagled on a tavern wall would be flayed alive while the throngs looked on and laughed and applauded as the victims' shrieks of agony rose above the babel of voices.

Yet, by some amazing psychological kink in their warped minds, the buccaneers felt that their hell-hole at Port Royal was not all that it should be without a church. So forthwith they erected a temple of worship, fitting it with the gold and silver vessels, the plate, the candlesticks—even the tapestries and paintings—looted from other churches. And as they were most thoroughgoing rascals in everything they undertook, the buccaneer leaders announced that, now they had a church, all must attend it. More than once Morgan and other chieftains promptly pistoled some tipsy fellow who interrupted the services, which—quite in keeping with buccaneer ways—were usually conducted by some unfortunate clergyman captive, who—so it is related—earned his liberty by preaching in the buccaneer's church. Of course Port Royal's religion was as much a mockery as its church, and never in the least did either influence the lives or behavior of the town's execrable denizens. Though it was openly and notoriously—even boastfully—a pirates' nest, it was winked at by the British authorities, and even encouraged as long as the buccaneers brought prosperity and trade to Jamaica and preyed only upon the ships, cities and subjects of the King of Spain.

And then, at one swoop—almost in the twinkling of an eye—Port Royal was wiped from the face of the earth, together with nearly all of its inhabitants. Without warning, with no opportunity for the drunken, roistering, bloody-handed fiends to repent their evil ways, the end came one day in June, 1692. A terrific earthquake shook Jamaica from one end to the other. Everywhere buildings were cracked and thrown down and Port Royal, with over three thousand of its buildings, practically all its people and with all its incalculable accumulated treasures, dropped into the sea.

Words cannot picture the terrible scenes that must have been presented on that fateful day, the crumbling walls, the toppling buildings, the terror-mad people fleeing wildly, blindly through the heaving streets; the blear-eyed, cursing pirates stumbling drunkenly from their kennels as timbers cracked and masonry fell; the panic-stricken men, blaspheming and swearing as they cut down all who stood in their way, intent only on escaping the tumbling walls, tripping over the bodies of men and women, stampeding, milling, until the struggling, fighting mob was overwhelmed and swallowed up by the inrushing water. Merchants and buccaneers, men, women and children, captives and slaves, harlots and sailors, guilty and innocent—all met the same fate; and only bits of wreckage, a few struggling figures and countless corpses floating on the bay remained to mark the scene of the cataclysm. Only a small portion—a fraction of the town—remained above the sea, the section where, above the limit of the devastation, Fort Charles still remained intact, still looking seaward; while overhead the buzzards wheeled and circled, disturbed at their loathsome feasts, presently to descend once more to the gruesome corpses swinging in the wind from their gibbets beyond reach of the waves.

Port Royal never was rebuilt. As a town of importance it ceased to exist after the earthquake, but it never was deserted completely; and, gradually, from the remains of the buccaneers' stronghold, the present settlement has come into existence—a village of narrow lanes and modest homes of colored folk, of a few stately residences with balustrades and balconies richly carved by long-forgotten men who chiseled many a ship's figure-head from oak or teak; a village of trim gardens and well-kept lawns, all centering about the huge barrack square. Of notable buildings few remain. There is the old courthouse flanked by arcades, a severe looking structure appearing as though during centuries it had taken upon itself the aus-tere, dignified character of the bewigged jurists who have sat within it; the naval hospital so typi-cally English and surrounded by such even more typically English gardens that it seems most in-congruous in a tropic setting. And of course there is the inevitable cricket pitch, the bowling green and the tennis courts without which no Britisher —nor his women folk—could exist.

But the once busy quays, or rather those that replaced the buccaneers' docks, are almost de-serted. The warehouses along the strand are al-most empty and contain only rusting chain-cable, bits of cordage and odds and ends. The sail lofts are bare, but near at hand is the naval yard with its many huge figureheads of famous old British ships and frigates, perhaps the most interesting objects in the entire town.

Taken all in all, Port Royal today has an inde-scribable but unmistakable air of resenting intrusion, as if it were communing with itself, thinking with half closed eyes upon the evils and the fame of its past, and disliking being disturbed in its retrospections. In short it always reminds me of some old roué dozing in the sun, his once smart clothing faded, shiny and patched, a faded flower in his buttonhole, his toothless jaw sagging, and a vacuous grin on his mottled face as his senile mind harks back to the gay days and scandals of his youth when decent people looked at him askance and his name was on everyone's tongue.

The few survivors of the destruction of Port Royal, seeing the error of their ways—and mayhap repenting of their sins—moved across the bay and settled on the site of Kingston. Piracy was abandoned in favor of honest pursuits; gradually the buccaneers were driven from the Caribbean; Kingston became an orderly city which grew and prospered, while great estates, peaceful planters, honest traders and merchants brought wealth and stability to the island.

Yet Jamaica seems ever to have been under an evil spell, under a dark cloud of adversity. Moralists might argue that the island's misfortunes were a manifest retribution for the wickedness nurtured and encouraged at Port Royal, were it not for the fact that Jamaica's troubles far antedate the days of the buccaneers. Indeed, its turbulent chapters began when Columbus arrived on the northern coast in June, 1503, and beached his leaky vessels at a spot now known as Don Christopher's Cove,* where he remained over a year, a year of hardships, suffering, mutiny and dangers, until rescued by ships from Hispaniola. It was during this period that he made his famous—even if probably fabulous—prophecy of the moon's eclipse, thereby saving himself and men from just massacre at the hands of the natives. Then, in 1655, the British invaded the island and wrested it from the Spaniards. The conflict, as conflicts go, did not amount to much; but its indirect results brought ruin and devastation with the loss of countless lives.

During the hostilities thousands of negro slaves escaped, and fleeing to jungles and mountains these runaways reverted to African savagery and became known as Cimmaroons or more commonly Maroons. With strongholds in the impenetrable forests and unknown fastnesses of the mountains, the Maroons carried on a pitiless guerilla warfare, burning the plantations, waylaying and murder-

* Although local tradition gives Don Christopher's Cove as the spot where Columbus beached his ships, historical evidence points to the mouth of Drax Hall River as the real locality. In all probability Don Christopher's Cove, as well as a second cove of the same name in St. Mary's Parish was so called in honor of Don Christoforo Ysassi, the last Spanish governor of Jamaica.

ing travelers, sacking outlying towns, carrying off
white women, torturing prisoners and committing
every possible atrocity. In vain armed expeditions
were dispatched against them, until, finding it
hopeless to exterminate the Maroons, the British
at last condescended to make a treaty by the terms
of which the negroes were granted their freedom
and were allotted twenty-five hundred acres of
land in perpetuity. But even then the whites were
not left long in peace. In 1760, the slaves rose
and, with African savagery, butchered, tortured,
burned and pillaged. Five years after this outbreak the Maroons again broke out and left a wide
trail of burned fields, smoldering ruins and mutilated corpses across the island. At last a second
treaty was signed and over five hundred negroes
were deported to Sierra Leone. Even after slavery
had been abolished in 1838, the freed blacks rose,
massacring the whites and burning their homes
at Montego Bay, while, for many years, the hills
and outlying country were infested by thieves, outlaws and brigands.

To add full measure to Jamaica's troubles, hurricanes and earthquakes have repeatedly devastated the island. Aside from the unimportant
tremblors and "overgrowyne stormes," as Captain John Smith called them, there was the earthquake of 1692 which destroyed Port Royal. Then

in 1744 Savanna-la-Mar was destroyed by an earthquake. In 1880, countless houses in Kingston were wrecked by a hurricane which took a toll of thirty lives and destroyed nearly all the wharves. A terrible conflagration swept the city in December, 1882, when over six hundred buildings went up in flames. On August 11, 1903, a hurricane caused damages of over ten million dollars, and then came the earthquake and fire of January 14, 1907, when over one thousand lives were lost and Kingston was left in smoldering ruins, while terrible havoc was wrought throughout the island.

And finally came that modern prototype of the old-time pirates—the gigantic trust known as the United Fruit Company. With even more convincing weapons, in the form of dollars, replacing the cutlass and pistol, and with white-hulled steamships in place of ornate, high-pooped, pot-bellied vessels bristling with guns, the Fruit Company obtained a strangle hold on Jamaica's chief industry—bananas. No one can deny that the Fruit Company rendered Jamaica a tremendous service in bringing money to the island—but so did the old buccaneers; neither can anyone deny that the Fruit Company erected much needed hotels, developed ports, increased business and made Jamaica famous. But the buccaneers did the same— aside from building hotels—and the presence of the pirates was little less inimical to the welfare of the island than was the monopoly of Jamaica's produce by the Fruit Company. But in time the more wide-awake Jamaicans realized the curse of being dictated to and virtually controlled by a grasping trust; and, with highly commendable spirit and initiative, they formed their own organization, known as the Jamaica Banana Producers' Association, and, figuratively snapping their fingers at the octopus, marketed their bananas as and where they saw fit.

CHAPTER II

KINGSTON, the chief port and capital of Jamaica, cannot be considered an historically interesting or an architecturally attractive city, and its climate is not all that could be desired. It is a hot and glaring town, and, as it was almost totally destroyed by the earthquake and the fire that followed in January, 1907, most of the old buildings it previously contained have forever disappeared. But it is a busy, progressive city, an important place, with a wealth of shipping, excellent docks, immense warehouses, innumerable shops; with tramcars and automobiles galore; with smoothly paved streets; with one or two really fine hotels; with the best harbor in the British West Indies, but—strangely enough—the most inadequately lighted city in the West Indies. In fact, after sundown, Kingston is as black as the proverbial pocket, for the street lights are woefully weak, few in number and far apart.

Still, compared with other Caribbean ports, Kingston is in most respects more modern and up-to-date, even if the various fires, hurricanes and

[23]

earthquakes, which appear to have had a predilection for Kingston, have left little of the old and nothing of the foreign or exotic about the town. And there *are* interesting things to be seen in the city, things which no visitor to Jamaica should miss, and a few days may be most profitably spent in seeing Kingston.

Although settled mainly by the survivors of the calamity that destroyed Port Royal, yet Kingston was planned and laid out by no less a personage than "Their Majesties' Engineer General," Colonel Christian Lilly, who erected the forts at Port Royal and elsewhere. As the "Engineer General" unquestionably was all that his title implied, he very sensibly designed the city in a far more orderly and more modern way than most West Indian towns, and followed Spanish rather than British ideas. The streets all cross at right angles, thus dividing the town into equal squares like a gigantic checkerboard, much like many of our own cities. And were it not for the fact that the Jamaicans have adhered to arbitrary names rather than adopt letters and numbers to designate the streets, Kingston would be a place in which one readily could find one's way about. But as it is the names must be memorized, and the stranger is almost as badly off as though the streets ran every which way. No doubt, to the

[24]

Jamaicans, the names of former governors and prominent men seem far more desirable than mere numbers as appellations for the thoroughfares of their capital, and we find such names as Beeston, Beckford, Haywood, Lawes, Elletson and Elgin Streets, all named after former governors, as were Nugent Lane, Norman and Blake Roads, Musgrave Avenue, Oliver Place and Manchester Square. Barry Street is named after the original owner of the land on which the town is built, and of course there is a King and a Queen Street. But I have never heard of a street, place, square, lane, road, court, avenue or even a mews named after Sir Henry Morgan.

Kingston is well provided with statues and monuments, the principal ones being that to Lord Metcalfe, at one end of Lower King Street; the Victoria Monument at the opposite end of the same street; the Dr. Bowerbank monument in Upper King Street; the Edward Jordan monument in East Queen Street; while, finally, there is the beautiful War Memorial in Memorial Square, erected in commemoration of the Jamaicans whose lives were lost in the Great War.

As I have said, few of the old buildings survived the earthquake of 1907. Among these is Headquarters House in Duke Street, the home of the Legislative Council, and the finest old town house in Jamaica. It was originally known as the Hibbert House, from the name of its builder, Thomas Hibbert, a merchant-prince of the eighteenth century. Another old building is the Scottish Church, built in 1814, which contains the bust of Rev. John Radcliffe, by the sculptor, Sir Thomas Brock.

Of the other churches, the handsomest is probably the Roman Catholic Cathedral, built after the earthquake, while the most famous and most interesting is the old Parish Church. The original Parish Church was the first church built in Kingston after the destruction of Port Royal, and, although it withstood the quake and fire, it was badly damaged. Its tower was split, its steeple was left drunkenly awry and its interior was wrecked, but its contents were saved and the Jamaicans very sensibly rebuilt the church in much the same style as before. Among its contents are the ragged battle flags carried by Britain's triumphant ships in the old days and the flags borne by Jamaica's sons during the Great War. Also within the church are many memorials to Jamaica's illustrious dead. Among them are monuments to Malcom Laing, Fortunatus Dwarris and John Wolmer, all by Bacon; and memorials to Edward Manning, Rear Admiral William Brown, Hector Mitchell, and Edward Jordan; while the graveyard of the church contains the tombstone of Janet Scott, sister of the author of "Tom Cringle's Log."

But by far the most interesting object within the church is the slab of black marble that marks the resting place of Admiral Benbow. Upon it is the coat of arms of the Benbow family and the following quaint inscription:

> Here lyeth Interred the
> Body of John Benbow
> Esq Admiral of the White
> A true Pattern of English
> Courage who Lost his Life
> In Defence of His Queene
> And Country November ye 4th
> 1702 In the 52nd year of
> His Age by a wound of his Legg
> Receuid in an Engagement
> With Mons Du Casse Being
> Much Lamented.

Obviously he who cut the inscription was no believer in punctuation, or possibly he did not feel himself capable of punctuating correctly and so decided to ignore such trifles and let each reader supply the necessary punctuation marks to suit himself. Having read the inscription one feels a bit puzzled as to just what interpretation should be put on the final line of the epitaph. To one familiar with the facts of the case it appears far more probable that it refers to the engagement rather than to old Benbow's "legg" or death, for the "wound in his legg" was received in one of the most heroic battles in the naval history of England and the sequel to one of the most disgraceful occurrences in Britain's maritime history.

The seven British ships, with over three hundred and fifty guns, met the French fleet of five large and four small ships off Santa Marta on August 21, 1702. It was a running fight, and had the British commanders acted in unison the engagement soon would have been over. But for some reason they held off, and, despite their admiral's orders, refused to come within range of the enemy. As a result, stout old Benbow carried on alone, fighting a single-handed battle against the nine French ships for four days. Each day he poured broadside after broadside into them, until his sails were in ribbons, his ship riddled with shot, his spars carried away and many of his men were killed and wounded. Then, through the night, he would heave-to and work like mad to repair damages and keep the *Brenda* from sinking under him, only to go after the French hammer and tongs when day dawned. Even on the morning of the twenty-third, when a chain-shot smashed

[28]

the doughty admiral's right leg, he refused to give in, but, while lying mortally wounded on a cot on the quarter-deck, he continued to direct the battle.

The odds, however, were overwhelming. No ship of seventy guns could vanquish the entire French fleet, and at last the indomitable Benbow gave orders to withdraw and head for Jamaica. Scarcely more than a wreck, but with her colors still defiantly flying from a splintered masthead, the *Brenda* headed for the nearest British port. And, despite his loss of blood and the fact that he was almost blind from the shock, the wounded admiral continued alternately to curse the French and his cowardly fellow officers, while over his head still flew the signal flags ordering the general attack which the other ships had disregarded. Arriving in Kingston, the admiral's leg was at once amputated, but gangrene already had set in, and after enduring terrible agonies Admiral Benbow died on November fourth.

Beyond doubt the seemingly inexplicable failure of the other commanders to obey orders was due to their hatred of the admiral, for Benbow was a most unpopular, in fact detested, man. Surly, rough, overbearing and even brutal, yet his bravery was never questioned. The disobedient captains—Constable, Wade and Kirkby—were court-martialed, Kirkby and Wade being convicted and shot, while Constable was sentenced to a long term in prison and died in confinement. Of the other officers, Hudson died before his trial took place; Vincent was suspended; and Walton, who had taken some small part in the battle, was exonerated. So it would not be surprising if the final line of the inscription on Benbow's tomb held a double meaning.

Of all the visitors to Jamaica probably not one in one thousand ever heard of the heroic old admiral or his epic battle with the French; and it is equally probable that there is not one in one thousand who has not heard of Morgan or does not know that the famous, or rather infamous, old buccaneer was knighted, and, as Sir Henry Morgan, was lieutenant governor of Jamaica. But the visitor to the island may search in vain for any memorial to Jamaica's piratical executive. Not a monument, a tablet or an inscription perpetuates the memory or the deeds of Sir Henry Morgan, and, in as far as Jamaica is concerned, the old reprobate might never have existed.

It is quite fitting that Morgan's career should not be kept green, for he was a most despicable scoundrel, a monster in human form, a beast if ever there was one, and fiendish in his cruelty. He committed the unpardonable sin of double-crossing his own men, robbing them of their share of

plunder and decamping and leaving them to shift
for themselves. In the eyes of the buccaneers this
was the most heinous of crimes, for, bad as they
were, unprincipled rascals though they may have
been, yet they were ever faithful to one another;
and only Morgan, alone of all the buccaneer leaders, proved false to his fellows. Had his robbed
and betrayed men been able to lay hands upon
Morgan, he would have had short shrift; and, instead of being sent a prisoner to England, where
he was knighted instead of hanged, and then given
a post of honor in Jamaica, he would have met the
same agonizing death that he had inflicted upon
so many helpless captives. Which would have been
no more than he deserved.

Morgan has become so famed as the epitome of
buccaneer leaders, he has become so well known,
his exploits have been so often told and so much
of romance and fiction has been woven about his
life, that the general impression is that he ravaged the Spanish Main and cruised the Caribbean
for many years. But as a matter of fact his career was very brief. He rose from an unknown
common seaman to the most famed of the buccaneer chieftains, performed feats that have seldom been equaled for bravery, dare-deviltry and
cruelty, was arrested, knighted and became the
Lieutenant Governor of Jamaica, and then van-

ished completely from history, all within the space of seven years, while all his notable deeds were performed within two years.

A native of Wales who had run away from home and had shipped—or rather stowed away—on a vessel bound for Barbados, Morgan first appears in the annals of the buccaneers when he arrived at Port Royal with several prizes, after a fairly successful raid on Campeche. Being a promising young scoundrel, he was selected by Mansveldt as his vice admiral when, with fifteen ships and five hundred men, the "hoary old pirate" set sail for an attack on Old Providence Island. Having taken the island and left a garrison of their own in charge of the captured forts, Mansveldt and Morgan sailed away for Central America, their plan being to land and march overland to the city of Natá in the present republic of Panama, and the oldest town on the American continent. But instead of taking Natá the freebooters were driven off with heavy losses, suffering one of the worst defeats in the history of the buccaneers.

Having "retired suddenly with all speed and care," as their chronicler puts it, Mansveldt and Morgan returned to Jamaica, whence they continued on to Tortuga. But before they arrived at that pirates' nest, "death suddenly surprised" Mansveldt and "put a period to his wicked life," thereby leaving Morgan in command of the old rascal's fleet and men.

After attempting in vain to secure the coöperation of the governor of Jamaica and various influential men in Virginia and New England, to further a scheme for establishing a buccaneers' headquarters at Old Providence, Morgan commenced preparations for a raid on Cuba. His first idea was to attack Havana, but ultimately this was abandoned and it was decided to attack Puerto Principe instead. This city, now known as Camaguey, was some distance inland; and the Spaniards, having received word of the landing of the buccaneers and their march toward the town, not only secreted most of their riches but had time to organize and form an ambuscade. Unfortunately for the Dons, however, the buccaneers arrived by a roundabout route and entered the city unmolested. Then followed the usual program—murder, rapine and torture, and Morgan, having for the first time full command, gave full rein to his cruel, bloodthirsty nature and bared his utterly depraved and inhuman character. At last, with everything of value he could secure by torture or otherwise, Morgan left the sacked and ravaged city. But when it came to a division of the loot, his amazed men discovered to their chagrin that the booty—according to Morgan's statements—

totaled barely fifty thousand pieces of eight. No doubt, in the light of later developments, Morgan falsified his accounts and put aside a tidy sum for himself over and above what was due him. But he was a glib talker and managed not only to placate his men but induced them to stand by him. With a fleet of nine vessels and four hundred and sixty men he sailed for his famous attack on Porto Bello, which he took after a desperate battle, and where he committed even more unspeakable atrocities than ever before had blackened the lives of the buccaneers.

By this feat Morgan had raised himself from an inconspicuous freebooter to the most famous of the buccaneers; but he was ambitious and planned even greater ventures. He therefore sailed for Maracaibo, captured that city and the neighboring city of Gibraltar, and spent five weeks torturing his helpless prisoners. Never had anyone, civilized or savage, invented such atrocious means of causing human agony as those devised by this Welshman. He made no distinctions of age or sex. He stretched them spread-eagled between stakes and beat them to a pulp; placed burning slow-matches between their fingers and toes; bound wet rawhide about their heads and exposed it to the sun until it shrank and, crushing the skulls, forced their eyes from their sockets; flayed them alive inch by inch; he had his men build fires upon the naked bodies of men, women and children; pressed them under slowly increased weights; sewed them in green hides and laid them in the sun; roasted them alive; mutilated them by cutting off hands, feet and noses; hung them by the heels until they died, and at last, with no more prisoners to be tortured, with no further loot to be won, and perhaps with even his awful lust for blood and cruelty satisfied, Morgan sailed away. Having twice accomplished feats hitherto deemed impossible, Morgan's next and greatest feat was his famous overland march and attack on Panama. There is no necessity of reciting the unspeakable and indescribable atrocities he committed, before, leaving the city in ashes, he returned across the Isthmus with six hundred prisoners and one hundred and seventy-five mule loads of treasure. Yet once more when it came to a division of the spoils each man received but a paltry two hundred pieces of eight!

But even silvery-tongued Morgan couldn't put over such a brazen piece of wholesale cheating as this. His men grew threatening, and Morgan— coward at heart that he was—sneaked aboard his ship at dead of night and, with a few companions of his own ilk, sailed away to Jamaica, leaving his cheated and despoiled men destitute even of necessary supplies.

Hardly had Morgan reached Jamaica when he was arrested on a royal warrant and sent to England, there ''to give an account of his proceedings and behaviors in relation to pyrates whom he had maintained in those partes to the huge detriment of the subjects of the King of Spain.'' But Morgan's oratorical ability—and his ill-gotten riches —saved him. Instead of being found guilty and hanged, he was knighted, honored and sent back to Jamaica as Lieutenant Governor. Possibly the King of England believed in setting a thief to catch a thief, for Morgan was just the sort of unprincipled scoundrel to betray his former comrades. He showed no pity for any luckless buccaneer who fell into his clutches. He was as great a rascal and as lacking in principle and honesty as he had been when a pirate, for the fact that he had been knighted did not alter his character in the least. Sir Henry Morgan, the ruler of Jamaica, was still Harry Morgan the buccaneer, as crooked a villain as ever lived. While he hunted down, prosecuted and hanged his former associates without semblance of trial, dispatched expeditions to Anegada and other lairs where they had sought refuge, and practically stamped buccaneers from the British West Indies, yet he was the same crafty, double-faced, black-hearted old villain of yore. While relentlessly hanging his old cronies with one hand, he was secretly financing piratical expeditions, led by his brother, with the other. But at last so many complaints of his dishonesty, his cruelty and his despotic administration reached England that Morgan was stripped of his position and was recalled to England.

What his ultimate end may have been is not positively known. It has been claimed that he lived and died quite peacefully under an assumed name in England; it has been stated on seemingly good authority that he settled in the American colonies where he was unknown; still another version is that he resumed his piratical career and was killed in an engagement, while still another relates that he was lured to a forsaken spot by one of his old shipmates and was spread-eagled upon the shore below high-water mark where he was left to die a thousand deaths as the waters slowly rose —the most appropriate even if least plausible fate of all.

But to return to modern Kingston and its sights and scenes. Among the modern structures that attract attention are the two rows of public buildings housing the law courts and other government departments and offices on both sides of

Lower King Street. Other notable new buildings are the offices of the Royal Mail Company, the Colonial Bank, the Bank of Nova Scotia, the Royal Bank of Canada, the Myrtle Bank Hotel and the Jamaica Club of Hanover Street. The former residence of the admiral of the station, in 1774, and now the almshouse, is of interest, as it was in this building that Lord Nelson was nursed back to health after his return from the Nicaragua campaign in 1780.

But the most noteworthy building in Kingston, from the viewpoint of most visitors, is unquestionably the Institute of Jamaica in East Street. The Institute, which is open to the public daily between 9 A. M. and 9 P. M., with the exceptions of Sundays, Good Friday and Christmas Day, is the real treasure house of Jamaica, combining as it does a museum, a library and collections of antiquities, old manuscripts, rare books and historical objects.

Unfortunately the museum collections, which are among the most valuable objects in Kingston, are badly housed in a separate building which was damaged but not destroyed by the earthquake. Among the collections thus badly provided for, and in constant jeopardy, are the splendid geological collection and the collection of birds, which includes several extremely rare specimens and a pair of the extinct Jamaica petrels. There is also the unparalleled collection of Jamaican land shells known as the Vendryes Collection, and a fairly complete and quite valuable archæological collection of the remains of the Jamaican aborigines. In the museum grounds is a miniature zoo which contains a pair of the now nearly extinct "conies," the agouti-like mammals which are the only quadrupeds indigenous to Jamaica and which formed the principal food for Columbus and his shipwrecked mariners; some live iguanas, a hawk's-bill sea turtle; specimens of the mongoose and a number of live birds.

It is the greatest pity that the Jamaican government or some philanthropic citizens do not raise a fund for a proper fireproof and earthquake-proof museum wherein the natural history collections could be safely displayed. Not only do such collections invariably attract the attention and arouse the interest of visitors, but, more important still, many of the specimens can never be replaced. In the earthquake and fire of 1907 the collections were badly damaged, and two subsequent removals have played almost equal havoc, especially with the bird collection. The scientifically inclined Jamaicans often express regret that the magnificent collection of aboriginal remains, which was the property of Lady Blake, should have been acquired by a New York museum instead of remaining in Jamaica. But lacking a properly equipped and secure museum upon the island, it is far better for science that such collections should find homes in institutions abroad rather than be exposed to the risk of injury, loss or destruction that exists under present conditions in Jamaica.

The main building, which is new and modern, is two stories in height. On the ground floor, is the public reading room and general library of over sixteen thousand volumes, from which subscribing members may borrow two books and one magazine at a time. Visitors who are not members may have the same privilege for a period of three months upon payment of two shillings and a deposit of one pound.

In the vestibule is a small collection of war material, while upstairs is the lecture hall, containing the History Gallery and the West Indies Reference Library.

The History Gallery contains about three hundred portraits (not all on view, owing to lack of hanging space) showing nearly every man of note in the entire history of Jamaica. Among them are portraits of Columbus, Penn and Venables, Sir Henry Morgan, Lord Windsor, the Earl of Carlisle, the Duke of Albermarle, Lord Archibald Hamilton, the Duke of Portland, Admiral Sir

Charles Knowles, Henry Moore, General Sir
George Nugent, the Duke of Manchester, Sir
Charles Metcalfe, Edward John Eyre, Sir John
Peter Grant, Sir Anthony Musgrave, Sir Henry
Norman and Sir Henry Blake. Among the portraits of celebrated naval heroes are those of
Benbow, Vernon, Rodney and Nelson, and in addition there are many portraits of Jamaica's
scientists, historians, legal men, ecclesiastics, merchants, botanists, philanthropists, medical men
and men of letters. There are also many old cuts,
engravings, aqua-tints and paintings of the island's scenery—the oldest dated 1766–70—and the
well known series of engravings made by Boydell
for William Beckford, the cousin of the author of
"Vathek," who himself made his fortune in
Jamaica.

Among the notable paintings may be mentioned
"Lord Rodney in action aboard the *Formidable*,"
by R. E. Pine, which was exhibited in the Royal
Academy in 1784. In connection with this there are
twenty-six engravings illustrating the historic
action which saved the West Indies for Great
Britain. Several marble, bronze and plaster busts
of famous men are also in this hall, while priceless
historic relics are the two maces, one bearing the
date 1753 and the other 1787, which were at one
time used in the House of Assembly and the old

Legislative Council. For many years the older of the two was supposed to be the famous mace or "bauble" which Cromwell thrust out of the House of Commons. Some doubt as to the authenticity of this has arisen because of the date. But it is well known that Lord Windsor brought over a mace for the newly acquired colony, and his mace was reputed to have been the "bauble" of the Cromwell incident. So it is not improbable that the date, 1753, may have been placed on the mace when it was repaired or refashioned.

Another interesting historical relic is a purse embroidered with the arms of the colony and used in the days when the governor sat, *ex officio,* as Chancellor. There is also a slave-branding iron, an old Spanish bell dredged up at Port Royal and perhaps the bell from the buccaneers' church, and a carved tortoise-shell comb and case of the year 1671. This is the earliest work of art known to have been made in the British West Indies, and was manufactured for Lady Lynch.

On either side of the History Gallery are arranged the seven thousand volumes of the West Indies Reference Library, together with, manuscripts, maps, and newspapers, many of them unique and priceless. Among these is a broadsheet of 1718, the first piece of printing done in Jamaica, and also a copy of the "Jamaica Courant" dated

1775. With the exception of an older copy, dated 1719, in the Public Record Office of London, this is the earliest newspaper in the British West Indies. The library also contains the first book written by a resident of Jamaica, in 1624; the first book by a resident of Jamaica after it became a British colony, dated 1720; and the earliest known Jamaican printed book, dated 1740. Another interesting feature is a series of almanacs, complete from 1780 to 1881. Among the newspapers there are issues of every year from 1780 until the present date, while the collection of Jamaica maps is the most complete in existence. Very few books printed in Jamaica or relating to any feature of the island are known to exist which are not included in this library, and in addition there is a very complete series of works relating to the other British West Indies and to all countries bordering on the Caribbean Sea.

And finally, most interesting and remarkable of all the objects in the Institute, especially to Americans, are the famous "Shark's Papers." These are the documents (written in German) of a Baltimore privateer brig. Chased by a British man-o'-war, the brig's skipper sought to destroy all incriminating evidence by tossing the packet of papers into the sea. Lacking the papers, the authorities could not prove a case against the vessel or her captain, and it looked very much as if the Yankee skipper would be released for lack of evidence, when into the harbor of Kingston sailed a British ship with a strange tale to relate. While off Haiti, Lieutenant Fitton had amused himself by fishing for sharks, and upon cutting one of the creatures open what should he find but the missing documents! We may be quite sure that the brig's skipper cursed sharks and piscatorically inclined Britishers with equal fluency and vehemence; for, solely upon the evidence of the documents so amazingly recovered, he was convicted and imprisoned.

CHAPTER III

EVEN if Kingston cannot boast of a great many local attractions and interests, it is, so to speak, the hub of the island; and within easy reach are innumerable interesting and most attractive spots. Excellent motor highways lead everywhere into the countryside; there are well equipped railway trains by which visitors may travel to nearly every portion of the island; there are coastwise steamers, and finally there are the bus lines connected with the various hotels in the country, with others running regularly between certain points. Speaking of the Jamaican railway, it may be of interest to record that the line was first opened in 1854 and hence is one of the oldest railways in existence. Today it is a government road and operates over a total of 207 miles between Montego Bay, Port Antonio and Kingston and to Edmonton and Frankfield.

No visitor on pleasure bent should remain longer than necessary in Kingston, for Kingston is no more Jamaica than New York is the United

[45]

States, London is England or Havana is Cuba; and all the greatest attractions and beauties of the island are inland or on the coasts. Within a few miles of the hot and glaring capital one may find cool, fresh air, charming scenery and delightful surroundings. Indeed, one of Jamaica's greatest advantages is that in a few hours—I might even say minutes—it is possible to find almost any climate desired. Thus, if the mean temperature at sea level is 78° F., one has but to travel into the hills and, at a height of 1000 feet, the thermometer will be about 75° F.; at 3000 feet it will not be above 68°; at 5000 feet it will be five or six degrees cooler, and at 7000 feet above the sea heavy wraps and blankets will be needed, for the mean temperature will not be far from 55°.

Even for those whose stay on the island is very brief and who cannot go far afield or visit the more remote resorts and towns, there are many interesting points within easy reach of Kingston. One of the nearest and most interesting of these is Spanish Town, the former capital of Jamaica. Founded by the Spaniards in 1534, it was called Villa de la Vega or Santiago de la Vega, and for more than three centuries it remained the capital; for, even when the island was taken by the British, Spanish Town, as they called it—the euphonious Castilian name being too difficult for Anglo-

Saxon tongues—was retained as their seat of government.

Unfortunately there is nothing at all Spanish about Spanish Town today. There are no crumbling forts with lanternlike sentry boxes, no low, massive houses with iron-grilled windows and cool patios, no blank-walled buildings with rows of arcades or *portales,* no outjutting balconies or twin-towered, dome-roofed churches. In fact Spanish Town is more like some quiet New England village than like a tropical town of Spanish origin.

There are the same grass-bordered lanes and streets and neat gardens filled with flowers; the same white-painted, green-shuttered houses, while the King's House, destroyed by fire in 1926, was a typically colonial building of red brick with white wooden columns supporting a heavy portico. Even the church—which is the oldest English cathedral in the British colonies—shows no traces of its Spanish ancestry. But this is not surprising, as the present edifice was erected by the British, over the remains of the original church, known as the Capilla de Cruz Rojo (Chapel of the Red Cross), or rather, I might say, over the remains of the remains, for the first church erected by the British was destroyed by the hurricane of 1712. The present building was built two years later, but in 1762 it was practically rebuilt and in 1817 the tower was raised, while in 1901 it was again restored and renovated in memory of Queen Victoria.

Of mellow pink brick, the church is surmounted by a lofty white steeple and is almost an exact replica of scores of churches in rural England. But within, it is a most interesting spot, for its floor literally is paved with tombstones beneath which repose the bones of all the most notable personages of Jamaica's past. Many of the sepulchres and memorial tablets are works of art by Bacon; many are ornate affairs covered with coats of arms and escutcheons, while everywhere are cenotaphs and epitaphs in both verse and prose, some of which are most quaint and curious while others are highly amusing. Thus, upon one tablet marking the grave of an officer who accompanied Penn and Venables on their conquest of the island, we may read that he "died amid great applause." Another, if we are to believe his epitaph, "came to an untimely end by just cause." This sounds rather like the senseless query: "Why does a mouse?" and leaves one consumed by curiosity as to what the "just cause" may have been which resulted in the officer's "untimely end."

As to the one who passed away "amid great applause" there also is room for speculation. In this respect it is very simliar to that other remarkable

[48]

epitaph upon the grave of Sir Thomas Warner, in
St. Kitts, which informs all and sundry that the
founder of the colony "boughte an illustryous
nayme with loss of noble bloode."

It is really to be regretted that the church does
not contain a tablet or an inscription commemorating the lives and deeds of the deceased officer's
more famous comrades, Penn and Venables; for
epitaphs of that remarkable couple, if inscribed
by the same hand that composed the lines perpetu-
ating the applauded demise of their fellow, would
be well worth the reading.

Invariably referred to as though they had been
business partners or a firm of solicitors, Penn
and Venables—never Admiral Penn and General
Venables—who took Jamaica from Spain and
delivered it over to Great Britain, were in many
respects the most extraordinary warriors in the
entire history of the British Empire. And they
were such an ill-matched and incongruous pair
that it remains an inexplicable mystery as to why
or how Cromwell selected the two to undertake the
conquest of the West Indies.

A man who much preferred writing treatises on
sportsmanlike methods of fishing rather than
fighting, General Venables was an ardent disciple
of Izaak Walton, and was the author of "The Experienced Angler." But when it came to battle, he

[49]

proved himself neither experienced nor sportsmanlike. The first time he went into action in
Santo Domingo he was ignominiously defeated by
a mere handful of Spanish irregulars, many of
whom were negro slaves; and, together with his
seven thousand trained troops, he beat a hasty retreat. And when, in company with Admiral Penn,
he reached Jamaica, Venables absolutely refused
to land troops until all the fighting was over! A
silent, morose man who suffered from chronic in-
digestion, Venables had more the appearance of a
medico than of a soldier, and perhaps even more
the aspect of an undertaker. According to historians he was in the habit of walking the deck
"wrapped in a cloak with his hat over his eyes and
looking as if he had been studying physic."

Very different was this angler-general's part-
ner in the conquest of Jamaica. Jolly, blond, ruddy-
faced and rotund, Admiral Penn would have made
an ideal Santa Claus by adding a white beard to
his features, and he looked far more like a good-
natured priest fond of the good things of life than
like the tough old sea dog he was. Very worthily
indeed did he uphold Britain's traditions of the
sea. Attacking the old Passage Fort, cherubic-
faced Penn, in a tiny galley, with a small party of
sailors, led the assault in person. Perhaps it was
the very dare-deviltry of the deed that dismayed

Roaring River Falls

Port Antonio, 1770, from a rare old print

The bridge crossing the Rio Cobra, from an old print in
the Institute of Jamaica

the Spaniards and caused them to surrender. But, whatever the cause, Penn's ludicrously impotent attack resulted in Jamaica falling into the hands of the British almost at a single stroke.

We might reasonably suppose that his country would have rewarded Penn for his courage and success. But on the contrary, as soon as he reached England, he was arrested and imprisoned in the Tower on the charge that he had returned without having first obtained permission! But he was soon exonerated and released. Then, in lieu of his share of prize money, he was granted a tract of land in the colonies, a tract which the admiral's son, William, converted into Pennsylvania.

The dour Venables also found himself in durance vile upon his arrival in Merry England—which was no more than he deserved—and within the confines of the Tower he had ample time in which to meditate on angling, the while pacing back and forth in his cell, wrapped in his cloak and his own thoughts.

Another curious monument to a past hero, which the visitor to Spanish Town cannot fail to see, is the statue of Britain's most famed West Indian sea fighter—stout old Admiral Rodney. On one side of the little plaza—for like every self-respecting Spanish city the town has its plaza, unless we deem it a common—stands an octagonal,

Greek templelike structure flanked by Ionic columns. Within this is a figure by Bacon which is intended to represent the famous naval hero who defeated De Grasse off Dominica and thereby established British supremacy in the Caribbean. If the redoubtable Rodney actually appeared in life as he is represented in the statue, there is little wonder that the French capitulated. Naked to the waist, bare-headed, clad in a short kilt and a Roman toga; with a short sword in one hand and a shield in the other, the Admiral would appear to be a Roman gladiator rather than a British sea dog were it not for his features. But these, being far from classic, make the effect of the statue ludicrous rather than heroic as intended, and cause the admiral to appear amazingly like a prize fighter emerging from a Turkish bath with a towel about his midships section.

All about Spanish Town are many delightful spots, the best known, as well as one of Jamaica's most attractive bits of scenery, being the famous Bog Walk. To many visitors the name of this favorite spot is a puzzle, for it is not a walk and there is no bog. But the explanation is simple. Under Spanish dominion Spanish place names were of course in universal use, and many of these still are retained, sometimes slightly altered but often so garbled that one never would guess their original forms. Thus Boca de Agua (Mouth of the Waters) became Bog Walk. Manteca Bay—so called because the chief industry of the local Dons was making lard from wild hogs—became Montego Bay. Agua Alta was transformed to Wag Water. Rio Hoja (River of Leaves) is now Hoe River. Rio Sombrio (Shady River) was corrupted to Rio Sambre. On the other hand, the British retained many of the old Spanish names in their original form. Thus we find Savanna-la-Mar, Rio Cobre, Ocho Rios, Rio Oro, Palisados, Trinidad, Port Antonio, Santa Cruz and many others; which is very fortunate, for, aside from a few crumbling bridges, some fragments of masonry, one church (of doubtful authenticity) and the old Port Royal bell in the Institute in Kingston, the Spanish names are the only genuine Spanish things that exist in Jamaica today.

But to return to the Bog Walk. Here the Rio Cobre or Copper River flows through a wild and picturesque gorge riotous with tropical vegetation, and in a series of rapids and falls plunges between its precipitous banks. But, as one visitor expressed it, the Rio Cobre is the most praised and most damned stream in Jamaica, for the loveliness of nature has been ruined by the dams of the electrical power plant, and, while we must admit the utility of these structures and the other obtrusive

[53]

evidences of man's having harnessed the Rio Cobre, still they do not add to its beauty.

Far more attractive—and still unmarred by man's handiwork—is the Stone Bridge or Natural Bridge about six miles from Bog Walk. Here the Rio de Oro flows through a deep cañon with walls meeting in an arch capped by a single immense stone slab sixty feet above the stream.

While Jamaica cannot boast of active volcanic craters, of geysers, of mountain lakes or of such mighty, sky-piercing, forest-clad mountains as some of the smaller Antilles, yet it has no dearth of scenic beauties; and prominent among these are its rivers and its cataracts. Indeed, the very name of the island hints at this, for the native Indian name—*Xamayca* (pronounced Shamayca)—means "A land of streams and falls."

Probably no one actually knows how many streams or how many cataracts are within the boundaries of the island, but it is safe to say that they exceed the proverbial three hundred and sixty-five. Many, of course, are small, many are hidden away and are not accessible to the average visitor, but there are several that are famous and are noted as sights that no conscientious visitor should miss; and, unlike so many of the "sights" which have been grossly exaggerated to lure the tourist, Jamaica's cataracts are well worth seeing.

Such is Roaring River Falls, a magnificent cascade one hundred and fifty feet in height and over two hundred feet in width; a roaring, rushing cataract in the midst of the tropical jungle. So surrounded by forest and palms and so interrupted by verdured rocks are these great falls that they appear like a series of smaller cascades, like a myriad dashing cataracts of a thousand forms, each lovelier than the next, roaring from nowhere to nowhere, leaping from the jungle above to vanish in the jungle below, veiled in prismatic spray and roaring with a thunder deafening in its volume.

Another famous cataract, and much nearer to Kingston than the Roaring River Falls, is Cane River Fall less than ten miles from the capital. Even on the hottest of days, the air in the deep gorge through which Cane River flows is deliciously, refreshingly cool between the precipitous rocky walls draped with ferns and trailing vines, hung with orchids and dripping with moisture. At the head of this entrancing cleft in the earth the river plunges over a lofty shelf of rock to fall into a great bowl-like depression rimmed round with giant ferns. Here one may pass behind the cataract and gaze out through the veil of falling water. And here, concealed back of the falls, is a deep cavern which tradition tells us was once the lair of a desperate and dreaded bandit known as Three-fingered Jack.

According to tradition, the triple-digited brigand was the West Indian prototype of Jesse James, "Robin Hood" and Dick Turpin rolled into one. Even making all due allowances for exaggeration and the romance which time invariably weaves about outlaws, Three-fingered Jack must have been a real "bad man," a tough hombre if ever there was one, and a most successful hold-up man, hi-jacker, knight-of-the-road and house breaker combined; a man who was far ahead of his times and whose methods savored more of the modern gangster and gunman than of the gentlemanly banditti of the King's High Road. Not only did he turn his mutilated hand to any phase of robbery; he was a callous rascal, and if a wayfarer who had nothing to steal came his way, Jack would promptly slit the unfortunate's throat for not having provided for a hold-up. And as he believed implicitly in the obvious truth that dead men tell no tales, it really made little difference to his victims whether they did or did not carry valuables on their persons. For a long time this charming occupant of the cave behind the cataract had everything his own way and accumulated a tidy fortune in stolen goods which he stored in his hidden den. But like most gentlemen of his ilk he came a cropper at last. In short he tackled the wrong man and caught a tartar in the form of a Maroon. A desperate hand-to-hand battle ensued, which ended in the complete victory of the Maroon who, as a trophy of war and to prove his prowess, lopped off the outlaw's hand with the three fingers and brought this incontrovertible evidence to the authorities. As a fitting reward for having done away with this scourge of the land, the officials presented the Maroon with a pension of one hundred dollars a year for the rest of his life.

We may feel quite sure that the half savage black man deeply regretted that the woods were not full of Three-fingered Jacks or similar brigands to be conquered; for the Maroons preferred fighting to any other occupation, and to win twenty pounds a year by letting the life out of a man in a lively set-to must have appeared the most delightful way of earning a livelihood.

Also within easy reach of Spanish Town or Kingston, and about ten miles from the former, is Old Harbour Bay. It was here that the Spanish under Esquival first landed on Jamaican soil; and here one may see the ancient Tamarind Tree Church, which it is claimed was built by order of Diego Columbus and hence is the oldest known relic of Spanish dominion on the island.

Even closer to Kingston than is Spanish Town,

[57]

there are many places to be visited which may be reached by carriage, by automobile or even by trolley cars. Halfway Tree, three miles from the capital, is on one of the car lines, and all along the route are the residences of wealthy folk who dwell in the suburbs. Two miles beyond Halfway Tree— so called because it is half way to Constant Spring Hotel at the foot of the Blue Mountains—the King's House is reached. This is the official residence of the Governor-General and is a splendid mansion in the midst of magnificent grounds and gardens. Among its other famous features is the grand ball room said to have cost upward of $25,000. After the great quake of 1907, the King's House was in sad shape, the only portion that remained habitable having been the bungalow of the governor's secretary. But the destruction proved a blessing in disguise, for, like all of the injured government buildings, King's House was rebuilt far better than before.

Also within easy reach by road or trolley cars are the Castleton and Hope Gardens. The latter, formerly the Hope Estate, and about six miles from Kingston, are at an elevation of seven hundred feet and cover two hundred acres of land. These gardens not only contain practically every shrub, flower, vine and tree that is indigenous to Jamaica, as well as innumerable introduced spe-

[58]

cies from all parts of the world, but they are so beautifully arranged in such a picturesque setting on the mountain slope that they are well worth visiting merely for their scenic beauty.

Farther from Kingston—about nineteen miles —are the Castleton Gardens. These are inaccessible by trolley, and the visitor must hire a motor car or carriage for the trip. For the first few miles the road is hot and dusty, hence an early morning visit is advisable. But as the road commences to ascend the foothills, the air rapidly becomes cooler; there is a most delightful breeze, and at Castleton—five hundred feet above sea level—one finds the climate almost perfection. Like Hope Gardens, those at Castleton are a botanical station which was established seventy-five years ago. Here, in addition to the wonderful display of strange and beautiful trees, plants and flowers, there is an excellent hotel and restaurant with bungalows and cottages for rent, and with arbors, benches and even bathing pools amid the beautiful surroundings.

Gordon Town, nine miles from Kingston, furnishes another pleasant trip. For much of the distance the road follows the Hope River, a brawling stream flowing through entrancing scenery among hills covered with tropical foliage.

Everywhere the valleys and ravines are luxuriant with greenery; flowering vines clamber over rocks and roadside bushes, and gigantic lianas hang like immense twisted cables over the verges of lofty cliffs. Neither must we forget the tree-ferns—most beautiful of tropical trees, perhaps—so abundant throughout Jamaica where they are known as "Ratta Drum."

Nearly one thousand feet above the sea, Gordon Town boasts a splendid climate and is a favorite residential district for many of Kingston's well-to-do citizens. In fact it is a mere village, consisting almost entirely of cottages; but there are accommodations for visitors, while all about are the alluring hills covered with coffee and cacao groves.

But to fully appreciate Jamaica's scenery, to fully realize the island's paramount advantage—the ease with which one may go from the baking hot city to cool, wind-swept mountain heights—the visitor should visit Newcastle, nearly four thousand feet above the sea, in the famous Blue Mountains whose very name is romantically alluring. At this lofty aerie the air is bracing and cool; northern plants, flowers and fruits grow luxuriantly, and one feels as if transported to another portion of the globe. Marvelous were the engineering feats displayed in the construction of the splendid road that leads by easy gradients to Newcastle, and marvelous is the view that lies spread beneath one's feet.

The capital beside the gleaming blue seems almost within stone's throw. Beyond the shimmering harbor, on which microscopic steamers creep, stretches the slender gold and green sickle of the Palisados ending in Port Royal—like the eye on the end of a peacock's feather—while to east and west are hundreds of miles of jutting capes, deep sheltered coves, rocky headlands and crescent beaches all rimmed with a silver thread of surf.

And if one is more ambitious and longs for even greater heights and more marvelous views and awe-inspiring scenery, by all means ascend to the summit of the range, to Saint Catherine's Peak a mile above the Caribbean. But even then there are still greater heights that may be scaled, and the hardy mountain climber, who does not mind a bit of roughing it, may reach the very tip of Blue Mountain Peak without difficulty. Loftiest of Jamaica's mountains, and the second highest in the West Indies, this cloud-wrapped crag lifts its summit 7338 feet above the sea. Here in the sweeping wind and drifting mist one has half of Jamaica spread in a vast map beneath one, a map of ten thousand shades of green, flecked with purple

[61]

shadows, cut by black gorges, checkered with plantations, orchards and cultivated lands; laced by silver streams and winding highways and set in a frame of sparkling blue sea. Or perchance a cloud eddies and swirls about the mountain top; the world below is hidden from sight, and one feels cut off, isolated, marooned in a boundless billowy sea of white in which the only tangible thing is the bit of rock on which one stands. Again the scene may alter. Beneath the tossing storm-wracked vapor, lightning flashes and thunder peals, and then, as the phantasmal sea is rent asunder, dark, austere, rocky mountain sides and streaming green hilltops appear as if by magic. Awed and entranced one can almost imagine oneself gazing upon the creation of the world, watching the birth of land and mountains from a drifting sea of nebulous, gaseous mist, and one half expects to see uncouth, misshapen monsters moving slowly about amid the forest trees below.

Upon this sky-piercing mountain top, the government maintains a small rest house for the shelter of those who wish to pass a night above the clouds; but, as the accommodations are most primitive, it is advisable to descend to a lower level, such as Whitfield Hall, a comfortable hostel four thousand feet above the sea and built two centuries ago. By a strange coincidence—and most appropriately—the builder of this house was named Heaven, and members of the Heaven family still reside (or did until recently) in this heavenly home so close to heaven.

CHAPTER IV

TOURING JAMAICA BY AUTOMOBILE

ALTHOUGH much of Jamaica may be seen and many delightful spots may be visited by railway, coastwise vessels, bus lines, trolleys, carriages, and especially by hired automobiles, the real way to see the island is for the visitor to take his or her motor car to Jamaica. There is not the least difficulty about taking a car into the island for a temporary stay. Cars are free of duty for a period of three months, but upon entering the country a deposit equal to 30% of the duty must be made. On foreign cars the duty is 20% while a 15% duty is levied on British made cars. If the car remains in the island beyond the three months' free entry, five per cent of the duty is charged for each excess month for six months. At the expiration of that time the full duty is collected. If on or before the expiration of the three months the car is taken out of Jamaica the 30% deposit is refunded.

No road tax or license fee is charged transients with cars, and special visitors' number plates are supplied upon landing. Unfortunately these bear the word "tours" which instantly marks the car

or rather its occupants as fair game for every
hoodlum, beggar and black gamin in the country.
In fact this is the only objectionable feature of
Jamaica's otherwise liberal attitude towards visiting motorists, and I know of several persons who
were so annoyed and pestered by beggars and
others, because of the tourist licenses on their cars,
that they became thoroughly disgusted and never
will visit the island a second time.

There is a Jamaica Automobile Association
which offers visitors a tourists' membership for
three months for 10s 6d. By addressing the J. A. A.
secretary, Coronation Bldgs, Kingston, full information may be secured, together with blank forms
to be filled out. This saves some delay in entering a
car. In Jamaica, of course, the British rules of the
road are followed—keeping to the left and over-
taking on the right. Today there are over 8000
motor vehicles in Jamaica, of which nearly 6000
are pleasure cars, so naturally there are numerous
garages, gasolene filling stations, etc. The roads as
a rule are excellent and the gradients easy, the
highest point on any road being a trifle over 4000
feet. There are two classes of roads: the government highways totalling 2337 miles and the paro-
chial or local roads amounting to 4366 miles.
Although the latter—like our own country or bor-
ough roads—are often in poor shape, the govern-

ment highways are constantly kept in good repair. These connect all the large or important places, and unless the visitor wants to do a little exploring in the more remote districts he need never leave the government roads.

Jamaican roads, however, are no places for speeding. In rainy weather they frequently are slippery and in good weather one never knows when donkeys, carriages or pedestrians may be just around a corner or on the point of issuing from some side road or plantation. Speed laws are enforced, the limit within any town or village being 12 miles per hour, while in the open country 20 miles is the limit set—though, as elsewhere, rarely adhered to.

To enumerate all the innumerable points of interest and the towns and villages which the motorist may visit on a tour of Jamaica would require far more space than can be devoted to it in this volume, but a brief outline will serve to illustrate the attractions the island offers and the possibilities of a motor tour of the island. Starting from Kingston a drive of less than an hour takes one to the Hermitage Dam (permission to visit this may be secured from the Engineers Dept. of the Kingston and St. Andrew Corp.) in a wonderfully picturesque setting 1700 feet above the sea in the

On the road from Kingston to Morant Bay

heart of the St. Andrew Mountains, and reached
by a road that winds like a huge serpent for five
miles up the mountain side. Here the Wag Water
River is held in check by a dam 700 feet in length
by 125 feet in height to form a reservoir covering
37 acres and containing over five hundred million
gallons of water. Other short trips are to Hope
and Castleton Gardens (already described), Bog
Walk, Spanish Town, Gordon Town, etc. But the
best plan is to make a complete circuit of the island, visiting all important and worth-while points
en route. Driving eastward from Kingston, the
main road passes Vernon, and the spot where Admiral Rodney watered his ships, by Rockford at
Harbour Head, Fort Nugent—the old residence of
Sir John del Castillo, first fortified against Du
Casse in 1694—and thence to Bull Bay. Eleven
miles from Kingston a road branches from the coast
highway and passes through Llandewy and hence
into the heart of the Blue Mountains coffee district,
following the route by Cedar Valley, Trinity Ville
and Serge Island to Morant Bay. Or at Serge Island one may turn off to the Plantain Garden
River Valley and Bath with its mineral springs. At
Bath the Gardens—a portion of the once famed
gardens of Nathaniel Wilson, a local botanist—are
maintained by the government as an arboretum.

[67]

They contain many interesting and remarkable trees and are far more typically tropical than Hope or Castleton.

If one continues on the east coast road, one passes Albion, one of the oldest sugar estates, Yallahs, and hence to Morant Bay. This was the scene of the bloody Gordon Rebellion of 1865, and portions of the burned Court House still remain. To the east are Stokes Hall—the oldest dwelling in Jamaica—and Stokesfield, the home of a colony of settlers from Nevis who were under Luke Stokes in the 17th Century. One has but to glance at the massive walls, the fortresslike appearance of Stokes Hall, to visualize the wild and bloody days of Jamaica's past when every planter's house was of necessity a fortified castle capable of resisting the all too frequent assaults by buccaneers, Maroons, foreign foes or revolting slaves.

From Morant Bay a road leads into the interior to Bath, once a fashionable spa, and rejoins the main road at Holland Bay. Just beyond here is Manchioneal, famous as the one-time home of Michael Scott, the author of "Tom Cringle's Log," and the scene of Tom's fictional attack of yellow fever. From Manchioneal the road leads through some wonderfully picturesque scenery, with the almost unknown Crow Mountains on the left, to the Blue Hole. This is one of the island's famed beauty spots, an almost landlocked lagoon so intensely azure that it appears more like cerulean dye than water.

A little farther on, the road enters Port Antonio with its fine double harbor, the west harbor being considered even better than that of Kingston, the two separated by a high peninsula. Although Port Antonio is an old Spanish settlement, and later, in 1723, became the chief town of Portland Parish, yet it was of very little importance until the development of the banana industry. Indeed, Port Antonio may truthfully be said to have been built on bananas and built by the Fruit Company. The most prominent building in the port is the Tichfield Hotel—a Fruit Company hostelry—on Tichfield Hill, which is the favorite residential section of the town, the business portion being on the isthmus. Aside from the fashionable—and extremely expensive—hotel, some fairly good bathing, and the fact that it is the most important banana port, Port Antonio has little to offer in the way of attractions. Fort George, once a stout defense and later a military barracks, is now used as a school, and the once famous sea battery is merely a relic of bygone times. But the scenery in the vicinity is most attractive, and as a center from which to make motor trips into the country Port Antonio has many advantages over Kingston.

One of the finest of the island's mountain roads leads from the port to Millbank, through Fellowship, Golden Vale, Windsor, Seaman's Valley and Altamount, with the beautiful valley of the Rio Grande on the right, the John Crow mountains on the left and the entrancing Blue Mountains beyond. At Millbank there is a most attractive bridle path leading through the Cuna-Cuna Pass to Bath, and at Seaman's Valley—so called in commemoration of the massacre of a party of sailors by the Maroons—the left-hand road leads to Moore Town, one of the original Maroon settlements and still inhabited by their peaceful descendants.

By taking the west road from Port Antonio, one follows the coast past the mouth of the Rio Grande, with magnificent views up the valley toward the mountains, and thence through Hope Bay, Buff Bay—where there is an extinct volcano—to Annotto Bay. At this point the road across the island from Kingston meets the northern coast road, traversing the island via Castleton, Scotts Hall—also a Maroon settlement—Temple Hall, Stony Hill and Halfway Tree.

Beyond Annotto Bay the coast road continues, through some of the largest banana plantations on the island, to Port Maria and Oracabessa (Oro Cabeza of Spanish days), the scene of Doyley's battle with the Spaniards in 1659, and thence past

White River to Ocho Rios. Here the road to Spanish Town branches off, leading through Linstead and Moneague to St. Ann's Bay, thus connecting the north and south sides of the island. The drive from Moneague down Fern Gully to Ocho Rios and past Dunn's River Cove with its splendid bathing beaches, past Roaring River with its famed falls, and on to St. Ann's Bay is one of the finest routes on the entire island. But to fully appreciate the scenery of the ravines and valleys —such for example as Fern Gully—one should leave one's car and proceed for a time on foot, for the top of a car cuts off the most alluring portions of the luxuriantly verdured cliffs, with their wealth of tropical vegetation, their exotic flowers and strange orchid growths.

It was at St. Ann's Bay, either at Don Christopher's Cove or Drax Hall River, that Columbus beached his worm-eaten caravels and made his famous—even if probably legendary—prophecy of a lunar eclipse. Also, a mile to the west, is the site of the first Spanish settlement of Sevilla Nueva or Sevilla de Oro. At St. Ann's Bay the Moneague Road joins the coast road via Finger Post. In fact, at almost any of the coastal towns, one may swing inland and drive across to the south coast or back to Kingston if one does not care to continue farther along the north coast.

At Dry Harbour are the famous caves on the Hopewell Estate, between Dry Harbour and Runaway Bay—the latter the spot whence Jamaica's last Spanish governor, Ysassi, fled to Cuba.

From Dry Harbour the main road across the island leads through Brown's Town, Cave Valley, under Bull Head and past Chapelton to May Pen; and near Stewart Town a branch leads through the magnificent Queen of Spain's Valley to Montego Bay, with a second branch to Ulster Spring.

Continuing along the north coast, beyond St. Ann's Bay, the highway leads through Runaway Bay, Dry Harbour—the first landing place of Columbus in 1494—Rio Bueno, Duncans, Falmouth, Trelawny and the celebrated Rose Hall, and so on to Montego Bay. Many persons consider Montego Bay the most delightful and prettiest spot in Jamaica, and in the old sugar days it was a very prosperous and important town. It is in the church here that the visitor may see Bacon's monument to Rose Palmer, who so often has been confused with the wicked and unfaithful Mrs. (Ann) Palmer of Rose Hall fame. According to local tradition, as related by the negroes, the mistress of Rose Hall—one of the largest estates on the island —was a sort of female Bluebeard who "killed she three husban's an' she fourt' kill she." Here also is the best preserved of Spanish remains in

[72]

Jamaica, Myranda Hall on the Falmouth Road, known as Miranda to the Dons.

Near here, too, is the Doctor's Cove, one of the finest bathing places on Jamaica's shores, while to the southeast of Montego Bay is the so-called Cockpit Country—once the resort of the savage Maroons. Although now peaceful and law-abiding, the present-day Maroons still live in a primitive communal manner, with a church, a school and a whipping post—the latter the most important of the three—at their central village of Accompong.

Inland from Montego Bay a road crosses the island via Montpelier to Great River, whence one branch leads by Chester Castle and Newmarket to Black River while the other goes to Savanna-la-Mar.

Onward from Montego Bay the shore road extends to Lucea, where it forks, one branch continuing along the coast through Green Island and Negril to Savanna-la-Mar, the other branch going directly across to the latter town.

Leaving Savanna-la-Mar, the south coast highway follows the shore to Bluefields, noted as the one-time home of the naturalist Gosse, who dwelt here from 1844–6 while writing his "Naturalist's Sojourn in Jamaica." Beyond here is Banister Bay, where the settlers from Surinam landed and where the survivors of the ill-fated Darien Colony found a refuge. Still farther on is Black River —perhaps the finest fishing spot on the island. The road then swings inland through logwood groves to Lacovia with its dye works. Here are two roads, one passing over Bogue Hill and through Mile Gully to Williamsfield, where it unites with the other road which passes by Spur Tree Hill and through Mandeville.

One of the most beautiful and delightful places on Jamaica, Mandeville, at an elevation of 2060 feet above the sea, would be a typical English village were it not for its palms, bamboos and other forms of tropical verdure. But it possesses something that no English village ever can boast—an ideal climate. It is a place of perpetual June, never too hot and never too cool, never too dry and rarely too wet. And no village in Merry England, and few anywhere, can claim a more beautiful outlook across oceans of tropical verdure, vast wooded mountain slopes and with the sparkling cerulean Caribbean in the distance.

Within a short distance are Grove Place, the government experimental farm; Oxford Caves, well worth a visit; Coleyville; Malvern with Munro College and Hampton School, and many other interesting spots; while for those who prefer nature there are endless forests, mountains, streams and

[74]

valleys to be explored with new wonders at every turn.

From Mandeville the road runs eastward to Porus, Four Paths, May Pen, with its sisal rope factory, and thence to Spanish Town and Kingston.

But before returning to the capital one may take many a short run to interesting spots. At the Alley in Vere is one of the oldest and most beautiful of Jamaica's churches. At Carlisle Bay the Jamaican militia under Beeston repelled the French from Haiti who attacked the island under Du Casse in 1694. Old Harbour Bay was visited by Columbus when homeward bound on his second voyage and near here are the ruins of Colbeck Castle, once the most imposing building in Jamaica. A vast pile over one hundred feet on a side, with four tower-like buildings three stories in height rising from the corners and connected by arched colonnades, with an outer wall with fortified towers at the angles and dungeons below, and surrounded by a moat, the place had the appearance of a mediæval castle!

The tour I have outlined covers practically the entire coast and permits several interior tours, but there still remain many fascinating drives, especially into the more mountainous districts.

[75]

From Kingston a main road leads past Matilda's
Corner (Hope Tollgate) and Hope Gardens to Gordon Town, where bridle paths may be followed
on horseback or afoot to Newcastle, Content-Gap
and Guava Ridge in the Blue Mountains. Or one
may follow the carriage road from the Cooperage
near Gordon Town through Irish Town and Newcastle to Hardwar Gap and down the Buff Bay
River Valley to Buff Bay, the return trip being
made via Annotto Bay, Castleton and Stony Hill.

Another new driving road extends over Guava
Ridge to Mavis Bank into the heart of the Blue
Mountains. It is in these higher altitudes, among
the virgin forests of the mountains, that the visitor obtains a true impression of Jamaica's fas-
cination, for when all is said and done the coasts,
the ports, the plantations, the lowlands and the
larger cities of one tropical island are very much
like those of another, and a tropical climate at sea
level is a tropical climate and nothing more. But
in the highlands the personality—if I may use the
term—of each island really appears. The "high
bush" of the Leeward Islands—of Dominica, Martinique or Grenada—are alluring, but are totally
different from the mountain heights of Jamaica.
The hills of Puerto Rico are not in the least like
those of Santo Domingo or Cuba, and Jamaica's
mountains are distinct from all.

Here, above the last of the great coffee estates, one enters the forest of giant trees; a forest worth millions could the timber be cut and transported profitably to a market; a forest of satin wood and cedar, of sanders and yacca, of bullet tree and cocobolo, varied by areas where magnificent tree-ferns fill the dark ravines. Everywhere, too, are the bamboos, forming their roof of delicate lace—giant bamboos with their great polished stems shooting skyward like vegetable rockets, climbing bamboos that cover the trees, bamboos so dwarfed that they are scarcely more than high grass—bamboos of a hundred forms, sizes and types, while here and there an obelisk of dazzling gold marks a flowering coratoe or maypole tree, or a pillar of vivid crimson or flame, a pyramid of magenta, or a mass of pink or dazzling white breaks the thousand shades of green.

Shady, cool, almost oppressively silent are these mountain forests. A tiny mite of birddom, a flashing, living, jewellike atom, poises on invisibly vibrating wings before a mass of begonia or wild plantain flowers and even the humming of the minute creature's wings are audible. An insect chirps in a tree top and seems almost to crash upon the stillness, and then from some dark shadowy dell issues the plaintively sweet, flutelike notes of the mountain solitaire.

Yet life is on every side. Graceful lizards skitter up the bamboo shafts; great soft-winged goat-moths flit among the shadows; gorgeous butter-flies flutter above clumps of jungle flowers; hum-ming birds flash back and forth; an unseen dove coos somewhere; dropping bits of seeds reveal the presence of a host of silent industrious birds in the tree tops; and the nature lover who knows the ways of wild things, and searches for them, will find that these silent solitudes fairly teem with insect and bird life.

Here in the mountain forests one feels cut off from all the world, far removed from civilization, from busy towns, from the rush and roar of in-dustry. It is hard to believe that within a few miles are great hotels, golf links and tennis courts, motor cars and afternoon teas, bridge parties and dances, railway trains and ocean steamships.

And then the spell is ended as the silence is broken by the tolling of a "budge bell" summon-ing the men to their labors on a coffee estate upon the slopes below.

CHAPTER V

IT was on his fourth and last voyage to the New World that Columbus, returning to Spain, drove his battered and worm-eaten caravels upon Jamaica's shores. Tradition tells us that the spot where his ships were beached was at Don Christopher's Cove near St. Ann's Bay on the north coast, but historical documents point to the place having been at the mouth of the Drax Hall River. However that may be, the fact remains that it was somewhere in the neighborhood of St. Ann's Bay, and here Columbus and his men remained for an entire year (1503-4) until finally rescued by a relief expedition from Santo Domingo. Although this enforced stay cannot be deemed a settlement in the true sense of the word, yet it paved the way for later settlements, for the shipwrecked Dons dilated upon the fertility and luxuriance of the island and the peaceful character of its aboriginal inhabitants. Here, to be sure, were no great stores of gold and gems, no riches to be stolen from the natives. But neither were there savage cannibals to be feared, no trained warriors

[79]

to be conquered. And in the island, with its rich soil and with abundant slave labor in the form of the friendly Indians, the Dons realized that Jamaica had certain advantages and promptly took possession.

To be sure, Jamaica never was really colonized by the Dons, as were Cuba, Puerto Rico and Santo Domingo. Instead, it was settled and cultivated solely as a source of supplies for Spanish ships. Indeed, had it not been for the fact that it provided a base for food supplies—and that the Dons feared some other nation might seize it if they did not—Jamaica would have remained neglected and unsettled for many years. As it was, the Spaniards established a settlement at Nueva Sevilla or Sevilla de Oro, on the north coast, and, enslaving the Indians, they proceeded to cultivate cotton, sugar cane, vegetables and fruits; and cattle, horses and hogs were introduced.

As early as 1514, Governor Garay was ordered to send supplies to Castilla del Oro (now Panama). Things did not go any too smoothly, however. In 1521, a pestilence broke out and the Indians and black slaves died by thousands. The authorities, deeming this to be caused by the swamps and creeks of the coast, decided to move inland, and in 1534 founded the town of Villa de la Vega (now Spanish Town) with a population of thirty Portuguese farmers, together with their families, a handful of Spanish officials and priests and a number of both black and Indian slaves. But the town thrived and soon became the most important spot on the island.

It was soon after this—in 1539 to be exact—that three famous men arrived in Jamaica en route from Cartagena to Spain. The three were Jimenez de Quesada, the conqueror of the Chibcha kingdom of Bogota; Belacazar, the founder of Quito and Popayon; and Federman, the lieutenant governor of Venezuela. Oddly enough the three had met most romantically on the interior plains of Colombia a few months earlier, and doubtless all had great tales to relate to the wondering husbandmen of Jamaica, to whom stories of El Dorado, Incan gold and the wonders of the great southern continent must have seemed like fairy tales.

It was about this time, too, in 1535, that the ill treatment of the Indians began to attract attenion and forced Queen Isabella to issue a decree that the Jamaican aboriginal slaves should be "assigned" to married colonists rather than to bachelors, "so that they may keep them and teach them and instruct them in the matters of our holy faith." But even this slight amelioration of their condition came too late to benefit the hapless na-

[81]

tives who, a few years later, had been completely wiped out by the pitiless Spaniards who treated them worse than dogs and valued them far less.

By 1581, the Villa de la Vega had one hundred free inhabitants, besides ecclesiastical and secular officials, a church, a monastery of St. Dominic and two hermitages—Santa Lucia and Santa Barbara —surely a plethora of religious edifices for a town of its size.

At that time living was costly—for the period— as all Spanish goods had to be imported from Cartagena, Havana or Santo Domingo, and the common people lived almost exclusively upon cassava and beef. Still, Jamaica must have been far better off than the neighboring Spanish colonies, for the records state that over four hundred Spaniards—citizens, soldiers, women and children, arrived, "naked, poor and terrified," from Puerto Rico.

Poor old Governor Melgarejo wasn't having an easy time of it by any means. He had already appealed to the King begging that he might be sent elsewhere, "where his services may shine more and he may be able to pay his debts"; and the sudden influx of the destitute Puerto Ricans added to his problems. Moreover, he had recently repelled —most gallantly—a raid by French corsairs and

A bit of the Bog Walk

Port Antonio

had killed their leader, a rascal named Olivos, and he lived in constant fear of threatened reprisals on the part of the dead buccaneer's brother. British pirates, under the Earl of Cumberland, were also troublesome and were seizing Spanish vessels off Jamaica's coasts; and, to cap all, the much-harassed governor found it impossible to collect twelve thousand ducats due him for his eight years' services as chief executive.

From the very first Jamaica seems to have had a remarkable attraction for piratically disposed gentry, and when Miranda was made governor in 1607, he reported that the island was much infested by pirates. Also, he reported that he was not surprised at the deplorable condition of the island, for the people were "indolent and lazy," there was but one town worthy of the name, the church was decadent, the native-born clergy "poorer than the people" and even lazier, and that "nearly the whole year is taken up in killing cows and bulls only to get the hides and leaving the meat wasted." He suggested that shipbuilding should be encouraged, and gave a census of the island which, according to his figures, had 1510 inhabitants, consisting of 523 Spaniards, 173 children, 107 negroes, 74 Indians (all that remained of the thousands whom Columbus had found a century before), 558 slaves and 75 foreigners. Regarding the Spanish inhabitants, it was observed that "all were of three parentages very mixed by marriage."

Still, Jamaica continued to struggle on, until 1648, when a prolonged drought caused much distress and many deaths. On this occasion a monk declared the calamity was a visitation of the Lord brought on as a punishment for "card playing in high places," evidently aiming his shaft at Governor Caballero who was an opponent of the Church. At all events, His Excellency took it as a direct hit at himself, and responded by calling the friar a "liar and dissolute monk" whose abbot, Sedano, was a "garlic eating clown." As a result, the colony became divided into two factions—Caballeristas and Sedanistas. In fact the feud reached such a height that Sedano and Caballero came to blows, the Governor very nearly losing his life in the row. The ultimate result was the removal of the Governor who was imprisoned in Cartagena where he improved his time and salved his feelings by penning a long account of Jamaica and his troubles.

During all of this period of a century and more that the Dons had occupied Jamaica, they had remained almost undisturbed, while wild and bloody deeds were taking place on every side and the history of Spain's supremacy in the Caribbean was being threatened. Hawkins and Drake, Preston and Summers, with many another, were busily extending Britain's dominions, but sparsely settled Jamaica was passed by. To be sure, Sir John Hawkins cruised along the south coast in 1568, and in 1595, Sir Anyas Preston and George Summers landed on Jamaica's shores. But they did not molest the inhabitants nor attempt to seize the island, and when in 1596, Sir Anthony Shirley marched six miles inland, he met with "such poor resistance" that with little or no danger to himself and his handful of adventurers he plundered the people, burned Villa de la Vega (by that time rechristened Santiago de la Vega) and, during his stay remained "absolute master of the whole." He was much taken by the island, declared it a "marueilous fertile isle" and said, "we have not founde in the Indies a more pleausant and holesome place."

His raid no doubt aroused the inhabitants and warned them of their danger, for when the English under Christopher Newport attacked the island in 1603, they were beaten off with heavy losses. Yet forty years later, when Colonel Jackson, with men from St. Kitts and Barbados, went a-plundering through the Spanish West Indies, he landed at the present site of Kingston and with nine hundred men marched on Santiago and "plundered it to their no small enrichment.'' Among Jackson's men were many who wished to settle down in Jamaica and make it a British dependency, but Jackson would not consent and sailed away, leaving the island still in the possession of the Spaniards. But not for long. In 1655, Penn and Venables arrived upon the scene (see Chapter III). No doubt, had conditions been different, the ill-assorted pair, who had made such a flop of attacking Santo Domingo, would have been equally ignominiously defeated at Jamaica. But fate and circumstances conspired to make matters easy for them.

The governor, Juan Ramirez, was "crippled in hands and feet" and unable to move in his bed. Proenza, the commander of the Spanish forces on the island, was nearly blind from some affection of his eyes, and the whole command and responsibility fell upon the shoulders of Cristobal Arnaldo de Ysassi, a native of Jamaica of Basque descent and brother of the Bishop of Puerto Rico. That the Spaniards capitulated almost without a struggle at what is now Kingston cannot be denied; but all those who took part in the campaign give Ysassi credit for most nobly if hopelessly defending the island to the very best of his ability. In fact, for more than five years, Ysassi managed to confine the British to the eastern portion of the island and maintained Spanish supremacy in the western portion. And had Bayona, the governor of Cuba, taken any real interest in the matter and had he furnished Ysassi with the supplies and men that the latter begged for, there is little doubt that the British would have been forced to evacuate Jamaica. The end came when, through the treachery of one of his own men, a man named De los Reyes, Ysassi was defeated at Ocho Rios whence he fled to Cuba.

When the island finally fell into the hands of the British, (being formally ceded to England in 1670) about half the population consisted of people of mixed Spanish and Portuguese descent, the other half being slaves, while much intermarriage of whites and blacks had taken place. They had many settlements, aside from their capital at Santiago de la Vega; among others being those at Caguaya (Passage Fort near Kingston), at Esquivel (Old Harbour), Guiacanes (Galleon Harbour), Parattee Hill, Oristan (Bluefields), Savanna-la-Mar, Melilla, Chireras (Ocho Rios), Hibanel (Buff Bay), Puerto Antonio, Sevilla Nueva (St. Ann's Bay), Guayguate and at Elvira, with a lookout at Port Royal or Cayo de Carena, as they ·called it. Aside from these settlements they had estates or *hatos* at Morante (Morant Bay), Ayala (Yallahs), Lezama (Mona), Liguanea (St. Andrew), Guanaboa, Guatibacoa (Old Harbour), Yama, Pereda

(Pedro Plains), El Eado near Bluefields, and at Cabonico near Savanna-la-Mar.

They had built a number of roads, one extending from Sevilla Nueva along the coast to Port Antonio, another southward to Santiago de la Vega, and another to Esquivel (Old Harbour). From here there was a road to Oristan and thence to Melilla and west to Punta Negrilla.

They had explored and named most of the mountains and rivers, such as Agua Alta (Wag Water), Rio Cobre, Rio Grande, Rio Minho, Rio Bueno, Rio Magno, Rio Nuevo, Rio de Oro, Rio Pedro, Rio Hoja (Rio Hoe), Rio Sombrio (Rio Sambre), Rio del Seco, Boca de Agua (Bog Walk), as well as the Santa Cruz Mountains, Mount Diable, the Sierras de Bastidas (now the Blue Mountains) and many other localities. And by the introduction of cattle, swine, sheep, horses, goats, poultry, coffee, cacao, indigo, cane and many other vegetables and fruits; and by the cultivation of cotton, bananas, pineapples and other staples, the Spaniards had prepared the way for the more energetic, more ambitious and more practical British who found Jamaica already well started on its way to prosperity when they took possession.

From the very first, colonists arrived in fairly large numbers, once the island was under British dominion. Even as early as 1656, before the Span-

iards had been ousted and while the British held
only a portion of Jamaica, over 1600 colonists arrived from Nevis in charge of Luke Stokes, and
settled on the eastern coast. Cromwell soon after-
ward offered special inducements to any colonists
who would come to Jamaica from New England,
and gave as his reason that he desired the island
settled by God-fearing people. But he also suggested colonizing the island by Jews, and, in view
of the later developments, the number of God-
fearing settlers must have been about nil. However, the New Englanders were shy of migrating
to the island. They had heard too many tales of
tropical fevers, Spanish invasions, Maroon wars
and negro uprisings to be attracted to the place as
a future home. But they were a canny, hard-
headed lot even if a bit timid, and instead of setting sail for Jamaica themselves they shipped
their goods and produce to the island and thereby
reaped great profits and established the famous
West Indian trade that brought such prosperity
to New England in later years.

After a short era of military control, General
Doyley was appointed the first British civil governor, in 1661. The second governor, Lord Windsor, arrived in Jamaica on August 11, 1662. His
tenure of office was very short, for he remained in
Jamaica only ten weeks, but during that time he

accomplished a great deal in the organization of the island and the establishment of laws. Up to this time the British capital had been Port Royal —if the tiny settlement could be dignified with the term capital. But in 1664 the seat of government was moved to Santiago de la Vega, which was re-christened Spanish Town and where, in the same year, the first representative assembly was held. At this time the island was under Governor Mody-ford who had arrived with 1000 settlers from Barbados.

One of his first acts was to have a census taken, the result showing that the population totaled 4205. But thirty-four years later—in 1698—the population had risen to 47,365, of whom 40,000 were blacks. Very largely the rapid increase was due to two main causes. First, the unsettled con-ditions in the Lesser Antilles whence many British refugees fled to Jamaica when their island homes were taken by the French—as in 1667 when six hundred arrived from Montserrat and in 1675 when 1200 arrived from Surinam when that coun-try was ceded to Holland. Second, the fact that Jamaica was the headquarters of the buccaneers. Almost from the first these gentry had found the island favorable to them. Governor Modyford was a great friend of privateers, and from priva-teer to buccaneer was an easy step with no real distinctions, and no sooner was the capital moved from Port Royal to Spanish Town than the swash-buckling sea rovers took possession of Port Royal for their own capital.

At the time it was destroyed in 1692, the city contained over two thousand houses and fully eight thousand inhabitants, or nearly one quarter of the total population of the island. Indeed, at that time the principal revenues of the island were directly or indirectly derived from the buccaneer-ing business, and the total annual income of the seventy sugar mills, sixty indigo works and sixty cacao groves then on Jamaica was but a fraction of the sum brought in monthly by the buccaneers. And even with the destruction of Port Royal and with Sir Henry Morgan as Lieutenant Governor, this form of piracy continued to aid materially to Jamaica's prosperity for a number of years.

During the heyday of Port Royal, Kingston was a mere village of no importance; little more than a collection of fishermen's huts and the homes of longshoremen, with ramshackle wharves and a thatched warehouse or two, for the entire trade, all the riches and commerce—as well as the wicked-ness—of the southern coast were concentrated in Port Royal. It was not until the destruction of the latter in 1692 that Kingston became a port of any importance. The survivors of Port Royal—or at least most of them—crossed over to Kingston and henceforward it became *the* port and grew very rapidly.

But long before that time many important events had happened. In 1687, the second Duke of Albermarle arrived as governor bringing with him one hundred servants and five hundred tons of personal effects. He was an utter failure as an executive; he injured far more than he aided the island, and most fortunately he died within the year. But his shortcomings were somewhat offset by his private physician, Dr. Sir Hans Sloane, who was a botanist and naturalist and whose report on the natural history of Jamaica is still a standard work.

In 1694, the island was invaded by 1500 French troops under Admiral du Casse, but they were repulsed and driven off by the local militia. Two years later another French attack was threatened by De Pointis, but the French hesitated and finally drew off without firing a shot. In 1702 Admiral Benbow fought his classic battle with the French off Santa Marta and died from the wound he received in the engagement (see Chapter II).

At this time, too, the island was fairly filled with scoundrels of all kinds, former pirates and buccaneers, convicts who had been shipped out as slaves for a period of ten years and whose time had expired leaving them free but without honest means of making a living, and hardened criminals who had received pardons in return for enlisting in the militia, while in addition there were the bandits and brigands of the interior, runaway slaves and not a few hostile Maroons. Considering the conditions existing at that time it is a marvel that the island ever amounted to anything, that it did not become a lawless, chaotic hotbed of vice and depravity. But little by little law and order were enforced, the respectable inhabitants maintained their ascendancy, and Jamaica grew and prospered.

In 1711, the western portion of the island was swept by a terrific storm which destroyed large areas of growing crops, the damage to Westmoreland alone amounting to over three million and a half dollars.

In 1718 the first printing press was set up in Jamaica and the island's first newspaper (a copy of which is preserved in the Institute at Kingston) was issued.

It was at this period in British colonial history that edicts were passed prohibiting trade between the colonies and foreign countries. Naturally this led to what we might now term bootlegging, and a clandestine and illegal trade was widely carried on with immense profits to Jamaica and other British colonies.

In 1728, civil government was established, and from then until 1865—when the rights were voluntarily surrendered to the Crown—the people of Jamaica made their own laws.

From 1730 to 1734, the Maroons again gave trouble, which was not settled until 1738, when a treaty was made with them and lands allotted to them.

In 1744, an earthquake and hurricane caused immense damage at Port Royal, Kingston, Old Harbour and other localities.

From 1756 to 1762 (with a short interval when absent in 1759) Henry Moore was governor, and during his tenure of office he commenced building the King's House at Spanish Town. It is of interest to note that after he left Jamaica, Moore was appointed governor of New York, a post which he held from 1765 until his death in 1769.

In 1760, the slaves revolted in St. Mary Parish and were with difficulty suppressed, and six hundred of the insurrectionists were deported to the Bay of Honduras.

In 1778, Governor Dalling fitted out an expedition to attack San Juan de Nicaragua, and among the officers who accompanied the forces was Nelson. It was on this expedition that the future admiral and hero of Trafalgar contracted tropical dysentery, which very nearly resulted in his death. (see Chapter I.)

During the administration of Governor Sir Alfred Clarke—from 1784 until 1790—Jamaica passed through a most unfortunate period. First, in 1784, '85 and '86, there was a succession of hurricanes and storms. During the first of these, every vessel in Kingston harbor was either sunk or badly injured, the barracks were blown down, many lives were lost and an immense amount of damage to property was caused. Following the hurricanes, there was a threatened famine, and conditions became so serious that, regardless of British laws, Governor Clarke permitted the free importation of food from the United States. Even then thousands died for want of sufficient food supplies, and in the seven years from 1780 to 1787, fifteen thousand slaves actually starved to death.

Soon after this, in 1793, William Bligh arrived on the ship *Bounty* bringing breadfruit and other trees and plants from the Pacific Islands for introduction into Jamaica. But those who welcomed him, and presented him with one thousand guineas as a token of their appreciation of his interest, little dreamed what Fate had in store for Bligh and the *Bounty*, which was destined to become far more famous for the mutiny that took place aboard her than for her service in bringing South Sea Island trees and economic plants to the West Indies.

About this same time there was a great influx of French refugees from Haiti, and the newly appointed Lieutenant Governor, Lord Balcarres, wrote to England as follows:

"On my arrival in Jamaica, in April, 1795, I found a vast assembly of French emigrants, who had recently fled from the horrors of Santo Domingo. They were composed of all ranks, qualities and colors. Many of the *noblesse* of France, numbers of ladies of the highest condition and consideration, accustomed to every delicacy and luxury, and who had saved nothing from the wreck of their fortunes, excepting their menial female slaves and a few trusty male domestics, who to save the lives of their mistresses had endangered their own—these persons formed one class of these unfortunate people. A multitude of slaves and of handicraft men of colour, with great numbers of brown women, formed another class. A third consisted of an immense roll of French prisoners of war of the most alarming description. These were confined on the hulks moored near the shore; among them bands of incendiaries who had been sent to Jamaica by the French Directory of Santo Domingo, through the medium of prison-ships;

[96]

the object of these people was to introduce themselves by bribery and artifice into the island for the purposes of destruction, conflagration and revolt; they were furnished with a profusion of gold, and had been too successful in finding the means of effecting their escape from these hulks, and getting into the interior of the island.''

Very obviously the ''vast assembly'' of French subjects was not a wholly desirable addition to the island, while the ''too successful'' incendiaries at large added another factor to the already too numerous lawless element. Obviously, also, the rascals were altogether ''too successful'' in carrying out their nefarious plans, for the Governor wrote:

''An attempt was made on the morning previous to my arrival to set fire to Kingston, and the combustibles were exposed to view. Shortly afterwards the town of Montego Bay was burnt to the ground. . . . Such was the first *coup d'oeil* which I had of this people at the period of my landing— the prospective was still more gloomy. . . . In this situation, and with these sentiments, the legislature of Jamaica would not discriminate, but passed laws, the effect of which was the confounding of everything that was noble and deserving with that which was vile and dangerous. To my understanding the duty imposed upon me seemed difficult, but extremely obvious. National honour and every sentiment of humanity dictated to me the propriety of protecting with firmness and vigour the first class, and keeping a most vigilant eye on the conduct of the others.''

The poor governor certainly had a difficult task confronting him and his forebodings were aptly borne out, for he states:

"I had hardly fixed myself in the seat of government when the apprehensions which had alarmed me on my arrival, respecting the unfortunate admission of some of these French into the interior of the island, proved but too well founded, by the breaking out of the Maroon Rebellion, an event which nearly lost to His Majesty this most valuable possession of Jamaica.''

Governor Balcarres put the case very mildly and conservatively. Not only did the rebellion come near to losing the island to His Majesty, but it resulted in a great loss of life, unspeakable atrocities, incalculable damage to property, and, when eventually put down, over five hundred Maroons were deported to Sierra Leone. Yet, despite all these internal troubles, the largest sugar crop ever shipped from Jamaica was sent to England in 1803.

Columbus Cove, St. Ann, the traditional landing place of Christopher Columbus who discovered Jamaica in 1494

Courtesy of George Pearson, Kingston

Rozelle Falls on the Rozelle road

Again, in 1805, the island was thrown into a state of terror when it was reported that the French planned to invade Jamaica. But the following year Admiral Duckworth put an end to all such fears by winning a most glorious victory over the French off Santo Domingo, and with his prizes came sailing triumphantly into Kingston harbor.

The year 1806 saw great changes in Jamaica. That year the irksome and long-standing restriction of trade between Jamaica and the United States was removed, but the advantages gained by this were almost offset by the abolishment of the African slave trade which rendered the planters dependent upon the increase of native-born negroes.

For the next seven or eight years no events of great importance occurred, but it was during this period—from 1806 to 1810—that Michael Scott resided in Jamaica and wrote his famous book, "Tom Cringle's Log."

With the outbreak of hostilities between the United States and England, in 1812, Jamaica figured more or less prominently; and in 1814 the British fleet, under Sir Alexander Cochrane, and the land forces, under Sir Edward Pakenham, met at Jamaica, after their operations on the Chesapeake, and prepared for their attack on New Orleans. The offensive was, however, unsuccessful—thanks very largely to the Lafitte brothers and their smuggler-pirate volunteers—and during the battle General Pakenham lost his life.

At this time the question of slavery occupied the minds of the Jamaicans, and arguments and feeling waged hot over the matter of abolition, the matter finally being brought to a head by the negro insurrection of 1831, which resulted in damage estimated at over three million dollars. Two years later, in May, 1833, the Imperial Government passed a law declaring that, from August, 1834, all slaves in Britain's colonial possessions should be free; but wisely providing that there must be a four years' apprenticeship to fit the blacks for supporting themselves as freemen. On August 1, 1838, total abolition of slavery took place in Jamaica, and a sum amounting to over twenty-five million dollars was paid the slave owners as compensation for the loss of nearly a quarter of a million slaves.

As a direct result of freeing the slaves, Jamaica's prosperity began to wane. Thus, in 1828 —ten years before abolition—the island's sugar exports amounted to 101,575 hogsheads. Ten years *after* abolition—in 1848—it had dropped to 42,212 hogsheads. The fall in the production of coffee was even greater—from 22,216,780 pounds in 1828 to only 5,681,941 pounds in 1848. Theoretically slavery may be all wrong; far be it from me to defend it; but economically, at least in the tropics, it seems the only solution of the agricultural problem. For various reasons, which I shall point out in a subsequent chapter, the free negro is never to be depended upon as a field laborer; and in the tropics—I am of course referring to the American tropics—he is the only man fitted by nature to be a field laborer. We may strive to explain the downfall of the West Indies and other lands by all sorts of theories; we may argue that they were doomed to decline owing to tariffs, over production, beet sugar, modern methods, competition—a thousand and one reasons; but if we actually face the facts, and do not let maudlin sentiment blind us to the real fundamental reason, we shall be forced to admit that their decadence dates from the abolition of slaves, and that freeing the blacks spelled the doom of the islands.

But to return to the important events in Jamaica's past. In 1837, the first steamship to visit Jamaica arrived at Kingston, and, quite appropriately, she was named the *City of Kingston*. A few years later—in 1844—the famous naturalist, Philip Henry Gosse, visited the island and for fourteen months devoted himself to collecting and classifying the island's fauna. The results of his researches were his "Birds of Jamaica," published in 1847, and his "Naturalist's Sojourn in Jamaica," published in 1851.

Realizing that it was impossible to continue with the native labor available, Jamaica arranged with India for the importation of East Indian or coolie labor, under contract. The first batch of East Indians arrived in 1842, but the experiment was not altogether successful and was soon abandoned. Then the Jamaicans tried Chinese labor, and in 1854 over a thousand Chinese were introduced. But they were even less of a success than the East Indians. Again, in 1858 and 1869, East Indian immigration was reopened; and in the latter year the indenture system was established, under which the coolies came into the island fairly steadily until 1895. For the next four years none were received, but in 1899 about six hundred arrived and at the close of 1915 a total of 35,933 East Indians had been brought to the island. Of these nearly twelve thousand returned to India when their indentures expired, and in 1921, when the Indian government put a stop to emigration, there were approximately eighteen thousand East Indians in Jamaica.

In 1845, the first railway was opened, a short line extending from Kingston to Angels, north of Spanish Town, a distance of about fifteen miles. A rather interesting incident occurred about this time. On behalf of the Royal Mail Company, Captain Liot left Kingston with the Crown Surveyor of the island, Mr. McGeachy, to make surveys of the Isthmus of Panama for the purpose of determining if it would be practicable and profitable to construct a canal, a railway or a cart road across the Isthmus. In his report Captain Liot declared a canal practicable, but stated that for a half century to come it would not pay and that a road or railway would be the only profitable means of transportation across the Isthmus.

In 1860, the first regular communication between Jamaica and the United States was established, a line of mail steamers being subsidized, thus opening a new market for Jamaican fruits. Eight years later (1868) the forerunner of the United Fruit Company was started by Captain Baker as a private line between Port Antonio and Boston.

During the administration of Governor Edward John Eyre a most lamentable and sanguinary event occurred at Morant Bay. This was the so-called revolt of one George William Gordon, a fanatical minister, a planter, a merchant and a politician who held a most peculiar influence over the local people. The outbreak instigated by him resulted in the murder of Baron von Ketelholt, the Custos of St. Thomas-in-the East, and the death of eighteen other colonists. As a result of Gordon's acts he was tried by court-martial, found guilty and hanged, and Governor Eyre was recalled.

Governor Sir John Peter Grant who followed, and who remained in power until 1874, organized the insular constabulary, reduced the island's parishes from twenty-two to fourteen, completely reconstructed the laws, established an insular medical service, public works and a government savings bank; opened telegraphic communication between Jamaica and Havana; extended educational and postal facilities; developed the Rio Cobre irrigation works; separated Church from State in Jamaica; and was largely responsible for the establishment of Jamaica's fruit trade, thus making his administration the most epochal period in the island's history since it had become a British possession.

Another very able and progressive man was Governor Sir Anthony Musgrave who held the office of chief executive of Jamaica from 1877 to 1882. Among the other noteworthy results of Sir Anthony's administration were the establishment of electric telegrams, a coastal steamer service, the purchase and extension of the railway by the government, and the reorganization of the botanical department. But perhaps his most important service was in insisting upon the importance of the planters devoting more attention to the minor products of Jamaica instead of putting all their eggs in one basket, so to speak.

In 1886, during the administration of Sir Henry Wylie Norman, many political and judicial changes were made, education received a great impetus, an excellent system of poor relief was established, and arrangments were made to extend the railway to Port Antonio and Montego Bay. By 1894 the Montego Bay section, a distance of one hundred and thirteen miles, was completed, and two years later the Port Antonio line was opened. During the same time many new roads were constructed, old roads were improved and many bridges were built.

In 1901, the Imperial Direct Service of steamers was established between Jamaica and Bristol, and the record passage of ten days was made. But owing to Jamaica being unwilling or unable to pay its share of the subsidy, $100,000 per year, the service was discontinued ten years later (1911).

It was during the administration of Sir Alexander Swettenham that Jamaica suffered the greatest calamity in its history when, in 1907, a terrific earthquake, followed by a terrible fire, completely destroyed Kingston with the loss of nearly one thousand lives and property damage amounting to over five million dollars.

And just as Governor Swettenham's administration will always be recalled in connection with Jamaica's greatest calamity, so that of his successor, Sir Sydney Oliver (1907–13), will be ever remembered for the rebuilding of Kingston and the reconstruction of the island's financial status.

In 1912, a terrific hurricane swept Jamaica and left fearful destruction in its wake. Then came the Great War in which Jamaica did her bit most nobly. No sooner had war been declared than Jamaica voted fifty thousand dollars for local defense expenses and made a gift of sugar, a value of a quarter of a million dollars, to the Allies. Everywhere throughout the island men of all stations —white, black and colored—hurried to join the British army, many even stowing away in order to reach England. And when, in 1915, England asked for troops from Jamaica, 122,233 men responded and *not a single man had to be drafted*. The first contingent to leave departed on November 8, 1915. From Panama, from everywhere throughout South and Central America and the West Indies, the Jamaicans responded to the call and over 2000 recruits were obtained from Panama alone. Eleven contingents, totaling 10,168 men and 243 officers, sailed from Jamaica overseas, and wherever they fought—whether on Flanders fields or on Egypt sands—they proved their fighting qualities. And that they took part in heavy actions is amply borne out by the casualty lists. Of the 243 Jamaican officers, 82 were killed, while 1019 men, or over ten per cent of the island's forces, lost their lives. Also, Jamaicans secured their full share of the highest honors for bravery and heroic deeds, for among them they received one Victoria Cross, 27 Military Crosses, 5 Distinguished Service Orders, 1 Distinguished Service Cross, 1 Distinguished Service Medal and 17 Military Medals.

As a direct aftermath of the war, Jamaica reaped great profits, and during 1920 top prices were secured for the island's produce; but it was only a temporary boom and depression followed in 1921. And, as if poor Jamaica had not been afflicted enough, a series of hurricanes swept the island; while in August, 1922, foot and mouth disease broke out among the cattle, putting an effectual if temporary end to expectations in the cattle industry.

With their backs to the wall, figuratively speaking, the Jamaicans, instead of being utterly discouraged, sought to discover the root of the evil times that had befallen. They had not far to seek to find one cancerous growth in the form of the monopoly of bananas by the United Fruit Company. And with wonderful initiative and common sense the people decided to throw off the yoke with which they had been saddled and themselves reap the immense profits that had been filling the pockets of the trust. To do this the Jamaica Banana Producers' Association was formed. This local association of planters and merchants controls over ten million bunches of bananas annually, and in 1928 awarded a contract for the purchase of their fruit to the Di Giorgio Fruit Company of New York, while at the same time shipping immense numbers of bananas to England, thus once and for all breaking the strangle hold that the trust had so long maintained upon the island's greatest source of revenue.

CHAPTER VI

UNTIL very recently pineapples, bananas, oranges, limes, lemons and grapefruit were the only tropical fruits in our northern markets, and those who visited the tropics for the first time were consumed with curiosity when they saw the multitude of strange fruits in the markets of the West Indies, and were overwhelmed with a desire to taste them all. As a rule, the experiment was not altogether satisfactory to the experimenter, for it must be confessed that to appreciate most of the fruits of the tropics one must develop an acquired taste.

Today, thanks to more rapid transportation, better refrigeration and the ever-increasing army of tourists who return from the tropics with the acquired taste for tropical fruits, the mangos and ripe figs, the aguacate or alligator pear, the sapote and other varieties of luscious tropical fruits are obtainable at most northern fruiterers. Still, there are many which cannot stand shipment, and even those that are sent north are, as a rule, the coarsest and poorest varieties of their kinds.

The banana, which in the north is known only

[109]

by the common yellow and red varieties, is known in scores of varieties in Jamaica. There are big bananas, little bananas, fat bananas and thin bananas; green, pink, yellow, cream-colored, orange, and speckled and streaked bananas. There are bananas with skins as thin as tissue paper, bananas that taste like apples, pears, peaches or even roses; and it is scarcely an exaggeration to state that a person may eat a banana every day in the year and never taste the same variety twice.

Next to bananas—and excepting oranges, pine-apples, grapefruit, etc., which need no description —the most important and commonest West Indian fruit is the mango. At mention of the mango many a northerner will snort and turn up his or her nose in disgust. "Stringy, horrible things that taste like cotton waste soaked in turpentine!" he or she will exclaim. "How can any human being eat such terrible things!"

But there are mangos *and* mangos, and there is far more difference between a poor and a really fine mango than between a hard, sour, green apple and the finest Oregon fruit, or better yet, between a puckery choke-cherry and a California ox-heart.

Mangos of the everyday sort, grown on half-wild trees, are, I admit, about the most unpalatable of fruits. But once try a really fine mango,

[110]

a huge, gorgeously-tinted orange and crimson grafted mango, or a tiny, round, rose-pink "mango-cherie," and unless you are mightily hard to please you will be a convert to mangos forever more.

In such a mango there should be no fibers; the stone should be small, smooth and free from strings or fur, and the rich firm meat should have no faintest trace of the turpentine flavor. To be sure, there is an art in eating a mango; but then there is an art in eating spaghetti or pie or even green peas. Some claim that the only proper way to eat a mango is to disrobe and get into a bathtub with the fruit. And unless you know how to eat the fruit this is excellent advice, for the chances are you will be in need of a bath after you've eaten your mango, so why not save the trouble and enter the tub before you start? But a mango *can* be eaten without smearing one's face, hands, clothes and surrounding scenery with the squashy pulp. There are several ways of doing this. The simplest method, which serves admirably when in the country or dining *alfresco,* is to roll and squeeze the fruit gently until soft—beware of breaking the skin—and then, by puncturing one end, sucking the interior dry as though sucking an egg. Another method in vogue in lands where mangos grow is to pare the fruit, and then, while holding it with two forks—like an ear of sweet corn—gnaw off the pulp. But the tyro will find paring a mango fully as difficult as eating it. Much the best method is that followed by the really sensible mango eaters. This consists of spearing one end of the fruit with a fork designed for the purpose, which penetrates the seed, thus avoiding all chances of a mishap, and then with a very sharp knife slicing the meat from the stone. These slices are then eaten by means of a knife and fork or a spoon—leaving the skin quite clean—and the residual pulp still adhering to the stone is gently and easily sucked or gnawed from the seed while it is held by means of the fork.

Another popular fruit in Jamaica is the sapodillo or nispero, a far from attractive appearing product, resembling a rather round, undersized, rough-skinned potato more than anything else. But the sapodillo or nispero, or naseberry as it is pronounced in Jamaica—which, by the way, is the fruit of the chicle tree—proves the age-old adage that one cannot judge the contents of a package by its wrappings. Within that rough brown skin of the sapodillo—no, I must follow Jamaican custom and corrupt the Spanish word *nispero* to naseberry; within the brown and uninviting skin of the naseberry is a pale greenish or straw-colored pulp that, to my mind and the minds of many others, is the nearest thing to nectar that ever grew on trees. Of course, as in the case of mangos, apples, cherries, melons and practically every other fruit known to man, there are all grades of nis—no, naseberries. If picked too green they will be lumpy and tasteless or even puckery, with a gummy sticky juice. If not fully ripened they will be hard, woody and indescribably horrible in flavor. Finally there are some varieties that are poor and some that are good and others that are best. But there is one fine feature about the fruit. It cannot really be overripe. In fact the naseberry is at its best when, to the uninitiated, it would appear to be rotten, when it is about ready to fall apart of its own weight. But then, I have known persons who could not stomach the best sapodillo—or naseberry— and who declared it tasted like "sweetened mud."

Let these hard-to-suits try the anona or custard apple or its next of kin, the cherimoya. As a matter of fact the distinction between the custard apple and the cherimoya is a very narrow one. The true custard apple is a slightly pear-shaped, whitish-green fruit with a reticulated rough exterior, whereas the true cherimoya is the same general shape but has a decayed-looking, brownish, blackened green or slightly red skin with a smooth surface. In both fruits the interior pulp is white, creamy and filled with small, shiny, black seeds.

The flavor? Well, honestly, that is next to impossible to describe; but the fruit must be of a good variety, it must be fully ripe and it must have been plucked from the tree at just the proper state of maturity to be worthy of a description. One lady, who became a veritable cherimoya addict, described the fruit as being like vanilla ice cream only better. But there is a slightly acid and absolutely indescribable flavor to a good cherimoya that puts it in a class by itself and that no ice cream ever could boast. However, I have known northerners who didn't care for either custard apples or cherimoyas.

The same holds true of that delectable tropical substitute for the morning cantaloupe or honeydew melon, the papaya, or as it is called in the British West Indies, the paw-paw. Perhaps there is no other tropical fruit, with the exception of the mango, that varies so much in quality and flavor, and even the finest papaya must be iced to be really good. Like the cacao and several other tropical fruits, the papaya sprouts directly from the trunk of its parent tree, which is a stout, upright, fleshy tree, bearing a crown of large palmate leaves, and which forms one of the most striking and conspicuous features of Jamaican dooryards, roadsides and fields. The fruit itself varies from round to elliptical, from green to orange, and from a few

[114]

Lucea the chief town of Hanover

The world famous Blue Hole or Blue Lagoon, near Port Antonio, Jamaica

inches to a couple of feet in length, depending upon
the variety, the soil, the locality and the care bestowed upon the trees. In many places it is grown
for the purpose of extracting the papine, a peculiar substance allied to pepsin which is contained
in the fruit, leaves and seeds. It is a powerful di-
gestive element much used in medicine, and there
is enough contained in the fruit to be most beneficial to persons suffering from stomach or intes-
tinal troubles. Moreover, meat wrapped in papaya
leaves becomes tender, and the natives go so far as
to declare that a tough fowl tied to a papaya tree
will become as tender as a broiler! But to return
to the fruit. Like so many delicious fruits and
tasty vegetables, the papaya has a rather musky,
disagreeable odor; but a really fine papaya is the
equal of any melon; in the estimation of many persons, far superior to any. Like melons, too, the
papaya may be eaten plain, with salt, with salt and
pepper or with sugar—depending upon one's personal taste. Some persons take to the papaya as
readily as a duckling takes to water; some acquire
a taste for the fruit; and there are a few who never
can appreciate it.

Somewhat similar in appearance to the naseberry or sapodillo, but larger, a richer brown in
color, and ovate or elliptical in shape, are the
sapotes. The meat is rather firm, orange, salmon

or even scarlet in color, and has a rather spicy, sweet and unusual flavor. These sapotes, which are really excellent fruits, should not be confused with the mammy-sapote or mammee-apples. The last are big, round, brown fruits looking like rusty cannon balls. The meat is dry, coarse and tough, but has a rich spicy flavor and is delicious when made into preserves, jellies, etc.

Another fruit that many people find most delicious is the star apple. There are two varieties of this fruit—the green and the purple. Both are of apple shape, with smooth skins, and should be very ripe before being eaten. Otherwise they exude a thick, sticky, milky juice which is a variety of rubber. The pulp is sweet—not unlike a green grape in flavor—and when cut across shows a star-shaped design; hence the name.

Another fruit that invariably attracts and interests the visitor to Jamaica is the cashew. The fruits, which are waxy-looking and very beautifully colored with yellow or crimson, are pear-shaped and slightly fluted longitudinally. But their most striking feature is the kidney-shaped seed which grows on the outside of the extremity of the fruit. Some varieties of cashew are quite pleasant in flavor, but as a rule they are strong in tannin and very puckery. They are, however, extremely cooling and thirst-quenching. In their raw

[116]

state the nuts are caustic and poisonous, but when roasted are delicious and are widely sold in our northern markets and nut stores.

Space forbids a detailed description of all the other fruits, such as the gaudy, red ackee with its papery pulp and black seeds; the ginep whose seeds when roasted taste like chestnuts; the waxy-yellow, ridged carambola; the passion-flower fruits or granadillas used in concocting cooling beverages; the sour-sop also used as a drink and for flavoring ice cream; guavas which not only are splendid for jelly but are even better stewed and are not bad eaten raw; rose apples—pale-salmon spheres which one may pluck from roadside hedges and which taste like attar of roses; sweet-cups and sweet-sops, pindar nuts and governor's plums, Surinam cherries and alligator pears—all these and many more, as well as blackberries, billberries, strawberries, grapes, melons, cantaloupes and other equally familiar fruits, are abundant in Jamaica, although, as in the north, each has its particular season.

Even more abundant and more fascinating to the northerner are Jamaica's flowers. Many are easily recognized—the oleanders, the hibiscus, the bougainvillea, the poinciana trees, the passion flowers, with many of our old garden favorites. But there are more which are entirely new, and they grow in riotous profusion everywhere. Stephanotis, thunbergia, gigantic-flowered ipomeas and convolvulus; poinsettias, and scores of flowering vines with the colorful blossoms of lignum-vitæ, cassia, ebony, cedar. And everywhere the crotons, coleus and other ornamental foliage plants, and the innumerable forms of air plants; the cacti, the night-blooming cereus, the splendid begonias, the countless species of palms, ferns and bamboos, and last, but most fascinating of all to northerners, the orchids.

Of the more striking flowering trees mention should be made of the anatta with its rose-colored flowers and purple pods; the West Indian ebony with its brilliant yellow blossoms that seem literally to burst into masses of gold after every shower; the pale-blue lignum-vitæ, the wisteria-like purple clusters of blossoms that drape the limbs of the bastard cabbage-bark trees; the golden candelabra of the coratoe or maypole, and finally the gorgeous purple pyramids of mountain bride. Of native wild flowers only a few can be enumerated. There are the red and yellow portulacas, the "kill-buckra" weed with flowers like buttercups and often called Jamaica buttercup; the pink shame weed; the red and yellow Barbados pride; the blue Jamaica forget-me-nots; the pale-orange black-eyed Susans rioting over fences, walls and stone piles; these and over three thousand other species of flowering plants, in addition to those introduced from all quarters of the globe, make Jamaica one great flower garden. Even among the orchids there is an amazing wealth of forms and varieties, no less than two hundred species being natives of Jamaica. But why attempt to paint a word picture of Jamaica's flora? The island's flowers, plants, fruits and trees form a stupendous floral exhibition that in itself is well worth a visit to Jamaica.

CHAPTER VII

WILD BIRDS OF FIELDS AND FORESTS

To MANY persons the wild birds of a strange land form one of its greatest interests and attractions, and in Jamaica the bird lover will find a delightful field for studies and observations. But he will learn with the deepest regret that bird protection was too long neglected and that several of the most beautiful and unusual of Jamaica's feathered residents are now extinct. Like our own Carolina paroquet, the once common and gorgeous Jamaican macaws were relentlessly killed until now not a living individual remains on the island, as far as known. It was much the same with the parrots, and of the fifty-one species of birds peculiar to Jamaica five are believed to be wholly extinct. Still, there is always the chance that there may be survivors in the more remote districts among the mountains, and the possibility of discovering such adds a deal of zest to the bird lovers' explorations of Jamaica's fields and forests.

Like that of all the West Indian islands, Jamaica's avifauna comprises many species confined solely to the island. And for an island of its size the number of species peculiar to Jamaica was large (fifty-one) while in addition there were eight genera known only from the island. But there are also a great many winter visitors and migrants, and among these there is a chance of identifying many not hitherto recorded. At the present time less than fifty-five species of regular winter migrants have been listed from Jamaica. These are composed mainly of the warblers, finches, waders and ducks. About forty-five occasional stragglers have been recorded, and the so-called "constant residents" amount to fifty-seven recorded species, making the total number of species known from Jamaica two hundred and eight, or, without the five supposedly extinct species, two hundred and three—a very large avifauna for the island and affording a splendid field for the amateur ornithologist.

The bird lover accustomed only to the birds of the temperate regions will find many extremely unusual and interesting forms in Jamaica. A few—such as the owls, the grackles, the doves and pigeons, the woodpecker, the humming birds, the flycatchers, the mocking bird, the vireos, tanagers, finches, etc.—are closely related to familiar species; but many of the others are wholly distinct in habits, forms and characteristics. Among these are the Jamaican tody, combining the characters of a kingfisher, a humming bird and a flycatcher condensed into a mite of green and red; the overgrown cuckoos or rain birds; the quail doves, the honey creepers, the spindalis, the feather-tongues, and others.

Birds may be seen everywhere throughout the island, and the spots most frequented by certain genera and species will be found very similar to the localities where one would search for related species and genera in the north; but there is one difference which is invariably the case in the Antilles. This is the fact that in Jamaica—as elsewhere in the tropics, and especially the West Indies—certain species are confined to very restricted areas and to certain definite elevations. A species may be abundant in one patch of woodland, or in one brushy field, and yet be extremely rare or unknown elsewhere; another species may be found only in a few trees in a certain forest, while on the mountain slopes a species may be abundant within a fixed range of a few hundred feet of altitude but never found either above or below that elevation.

Also, even species confined to Jamaica, or residents of the island, may be common at one season or during one month and may disappear completely at other times; and at certain hours of the day certain birds may be seen which cannot be observed a few hours earlier or later.

Of course there are many species which are always in evidence. Thus, along the shores and rivers, there are always the herons, waders and sea birds. Prominent among them are the laughing gulls, royal terns, Cabot's terns, brown pelicans, frigate birds, noddy terns, boobies and sooty terns; the various herons, prominent among which are the blue and white phases of the little blue heron, the yellow-crowned night herons, the great blue herons and the West Indian green herons, with an occasional egret. White ibis are common in many localities; gallinules and kingfishers are usually visible in such localities as Bog Walk and Wag Water, and the anis, mocking birds, grass quits, flycatchers, honey creepers and vultures, as well as ground-doves, are seen at every turn.

Even in the trees and shrubbery in Kingston many birds may be observed, especially during migrations. Flocks of tinkling grackles, the common petchary, palm swifts, quits, warblers, vireos, humming birds and swallows are usually abundant in and about the capital. Farther back among the foothills may be seen the foolish petchary, appearing much like an overgrown crested flycatcher, banana birds or Jamaican orioles, several species

[123]

of grass quits, and other species. One of the best localities for observing the bird life near Kingston are the Hope Gardens. Here the long-tailed, mango and tiny vervain humming birds are abundant, as are many of our northern warblers—yellowthroats, redstarts, pine and palm warblers, black and white, magnolia, and, usually, many Cape May warblers, as well as oven birds and water thrushes. And here, too, one may now and then see a Jamaican tody, although this odd creature is far more abundant at higher elevations among the hills, where he loves to sit motionless upon a twig, head drawn back, ridiculous red bill uptilted, and every few moments darting out to capture some passing insect. As a rule, todies are most unsuspicious birds and will allow a person to approach within a few feet. In fact, on one occasion, while I was bird collecting, one of the queer birds actually selected my gun barrel for a perch! To find such birds as the jabbering crow, Hill's mocking bird, the parrots and the arrow-headed warbler, one must go farther afield into the less frequented mountain districts.

At Mandeville, many birds are common which rarely are seen elsewhere. Among these are the savanna bird, the Jamaican subspecies of our yellow-winged sparrow, the euphonias, spindalis, the becards, pottoos and other species, besides many migratory birds. Another rich bird district is the vicinity of St. Ann's Bay and about Ewarton. In such districts one finds the black becard, the thrushes, the Jamaica bullfinch or coffee bird, the various doves and pigeons, etc. At and about Newcastle, and slightly higher on the mountain sides, one may be lucky enough to catch a glimpse of the solitaire; and one is almost certain to hear its hauntingly sweet, plaintive, flutelike notes issuing from the depths of some dark, damp forest ravine. It is in such spots also—in the forests of the higher mountains—that, if anywhere, one may hope to catch glimpses of the Jamaican parrots and the jabbering crows.

And do not be disappointed if, after weeks of exploring and patient searching, you have not succeeded in seeing such species as the Jamaican spindalis, the euphonia or even a crested quail dove. I have at times hunted for more than a month to find the spindalis multicolor of Santo Domingo, and then suddenly have discovered scores of the bird feeding in a tree I had passed dozens of times. Yet, a few days later, every specimen had vanished completely. The same is true of the euphonias, which will swarm in certain trees, feeding upon the fruit, for a few days, and then may disappear as if exterminated. Quail doves also appear and vanish from a particular locality,

[125]

dependent probably upon some food supply: while, in order to study parrots, it is only necessary to find their favorite food and wait beneath the trees which bear it.

Perhaps the most unfortunate event in the history of Jamaica—as far as the avifauna is concerned—was the introduction of the mongoose. Brought in for the purpose of destroying rats, the mongoose not only killed off the rodents, but proceeded to destroy lizards, harmless snakes, the native coney or agouti, and every species of ground-loving bird upon the island. Such species as the quail and ground doves, the thrushes, the goatsuckers, and various finches were the chief sufferers, and it is only a question of a few years more before every ground-loving and ground-nesting bird in Jamaica will have gone the way of the macaws and the Jamaican petrel.

Before going afield in Jamaica the bird lover cannot do better than to secure a copy of Dr. P. L. Sclater's "Revised List of the Birds of Jamaica," which was published in the "Handbook of Jamaica" for 1920, and which is available in the Institute of Jamaica Library. "The Birds of Jamaica," by Philip Gosse, published in 1847, will also be found valuable, especially as regards the species now extinct.

For the benefit of those who may be interested in

the birds peculiar to Jamaica the following list is given.

Jamaican petrel (Blue Mountain duck) Pterodroma jamaicensis. Believed extinct. A pair may be seen in the Institute of Jamaica and there are specimens in the British Museum, the American Museum of Natural History in New York; in the Natural History Museum of Cambridge and the Museum of Comparative Zoölogy at Cambridge, Mass.

Jamaican clapper-rail (Mangrove Hen)	(*Rallus longirostris caribaeus*)
Crested quail-dove (Mountain witch)	(*Geotrygon versicolor*)
White-bellied dove	(*Leptotitla jamaicensis jamaicansis*)
Jamaican Ground dove	(*Chaemepelia passerina jamaicensis*)
Blue dove (Blue partridge)	(*Zenaida plumbea*)
Ring-tailed pigeon	(*Chloroenas caribea*)
Jamaican pigeon (Blue pigeon)	(*Chloroenas inornata exigua*)
Gosse's macaw	(*Ara gossei*)
Red-headed green macaw.	(*Ara erythrocephala*)

(Not a single specimen of either macaw is known to be in existence in any collection in the world)

Jamaican paroquet	(*Eupsittula nana*)
Black-billed parrot	(*Amazona agilis*)
Yellow-billed parrot	(*Amazona collaria*)

Jamaican lizard cuckoo	(*Saurothera vitula*)
Rain bird (Old man bird)	(*Hyetornis pluvialis*)
Jamaican eared owl	(*Pseudoscops grammicus*)
Jamaican potoo	(*Myctibius griseus jamaicensis*)
Jamaican goatsucker	(*Siphonorhis americana*)
Jamaican tody	(*Todus todus*)
Jamaican woodpecker	(*Centurus radiolatus*)
Vervain humming bird	(*Mellisuga minima*)
Mango humming bird	(*Anthracothorax mango*)
Streamer-tailed humming bird	(*Aithurus polytmus*)
Black-billed streamertail	(*Aithurus scitulus*)
Gosse's flycatcher	(*Hylonax validus*)
Black becard (Mountain Dick) (Judy)	(*Platypsaris niger*)
Jamaican petchary	(*Tolmarchus jamaicensis*)
Stolid flycatcher	(*Myiarchus stolidus*)
Sad flycatcher	(*Myiarchus barbirostris*)
Jamaican wood pewee	(*Blacicus pallidus*)
Sclater's flycatcher	(*Eleania jallax*)
Cotta flycatcher	(*Myiopagis cotta*)
Hill's mocking bird	(*Mimus gundlachii hillii*)
White chinned thrush (Hopping Dick)	(*Haplocichla aurantia*)
White-eyed thrush (Glass eye)	(*Planesticus jamaicensis*)

[128]

Jamaican crow (Jabbering crow)	(*Corvus jamaicensis*)
Osburn's vireo	(*Laletes osburni*)
Jamaican vireo (Sewy-sewy)	(*Vireo modestus*)
Gosse's swallow (Golden swallow)	(*Lamprochelidon euchrysea*)
Arrow-headed warbler	(*Dendroica pharetra*)
Aurora warbler	(*Dendroica eoa*)
Jamaican honey creeper (Banana quit)	(*Coereba flaveola*)
Orange quit (Feather-tongue)	(*Euneornis campestris*)
Osburn's blackbird	(*Nesopsar nigerrimus*)
Jamaican oriole (Banana-bird)	(*Icterus leucopteryx*)
Jamaican grackle (Tinkling grackle)	(*Holoquiscalus jamaicensis jamaicensis*)
Jamaican spindalis (Orange bird)	(*Spindalis nigricephala*)
Blue quit	(*Pyrrhuphonia jamaica*)
Jamaican bullfinch (Coffee bird)	(*Pyrrhulgagra violacea ruficollis*)
Yellow-backed finch	(*Loxipasser anoxanthus*)
Jamaican yellow-winged sparrow (Grass pink)	(*Ammodramus savannarum savannarum*)

CHAPTER VIII

THE JAMAICAN NEGROES AND THEIR WAYS

The northerner—who has not dwelt in the West Indies—usually throws up his hands in holy horror when he learns that the negroes are so greatly in the majority in Jamaica and elsewhere in the Antilles. He judges all blacks and colored people by those with whom he is familiar in the north, and he pictures Jamaica—with ninety-five per cent of its population of African or partly African descent—as an impossible place for a white man; a land of "niggers"; a spot where filth, laziness, sloth, viciousness, vile crimes, thievery, Voodooism and Obeah are rampant. And here let me digress long enough to point out the erroneous ideas that most persons possess in respect to Voodooism and Obeah. In the minds of most, the two terms are synonymous and imply some heathenish form of pagan religion in which human sacrifices and cannibalism play important parts. This is not at all the truth. Voodooism and Obeah are totally distinct, their only feature in common being that both were introduced from Africa.

Rafting on the Rio Grande, near Port Antonio, provides
keen enjoyment and mild excitement

Going to market in Jamaica

On the road to Monegue

Voodooism is a form of religion, a devil-worship, which in its extreme form *does* demand human sacrifice. But as practised in the West Indies—and it is far from common, except in Haiti —a kid or lamb usually is substituted for the human victim of sacrifice, although in Haiti human sacrifices and succeeding cannibalism are sometimes carried out.

Obeah, on the other hand, has nothing to do with religion or worship. It is purely witchcraft or sorcery practised by certain persons reputed to be "Obeah men" or "Obeah women," or in other words Witch Doctors. Unquestionably many of these individuals *do* possess a certain amount of hypnotic power, and the power of auto-suggestion. But very largely they depend upon the superstitious fears of the credulous colored people, hokuspokus, mummery and, if all else fails, poison. They are in no small demand by both blacks and whites in those islands where Obeah flourishes—as in the French West Indies and the islands formerly French, such as Dominica, St. Lucia, St. Vincent, Grenada, etc.—their services being sought, and paid for,—for the purpose of keeping trespassers off properties, preventing theft of fruit and produce, locating stolen or missing articles, etc., while many otherwise intelligent and educated merchants do not hesitate to consult them on business

matters, exactly as our own people patronize clair-
voyants.

And, as the ignorant and superstitious blacks
have absolute faith in Obeah and the occult powers
of the Obeah men and women, their "spells" and
nostrums are just as effective as if they actually
did possess the powers attributed to them. I have
known of West Indian negroes actually dying,
merely because some Obeah man had told them
they were marked for death. But there is a blacker
side to it. If all else fails to bring a desired result,
the Obeah practitioners do not hesitate to employ
poisons; and they possess an almost uncanny
knowledge of vegetable poisons and drugs. Finally, in order to work some of their "spells" and
charms, certain portions of the human anatomy
are deemed essential; and murders of children,
for the purpose of securing their internal organs
for Obeah, are far commoner than is generally
supposed.

Wherever there are ignorant negroes, there we
will find a certain amount of Obeah; but it is far
more prevalent in some places than in others, and
there is far less of it—and in a far milder form—
in Jamaica than in Cuba or Haiti or the Lesser
Antilles.

And when the northerner judges the West Indian colored or black man by his fellows of the

north, he does the former a rank injustice. Even if
the West Indian negro, when transplanted to New
York or elsewhere in the States, is little better
than the American-born negro, he is a very distinct and very superior type in his own land. In
the first place, his ancestors were derived from a
different section of Africa; and in the second place
he and his forbears have been bred, reared and
educated in a totally different way and under a
wholly different environment.

To be sure, the character of the negro varies
somewhat in the different islands, but during over
thirty years' experience in the West Indies, and
after having dwelt on every West Indian island, I
can truthfully say that I do not know of a single
British, Dutch or French West Indian island
where the colored population can be considered
vicious, lawless or dangerous. I do not know of
any British West Indian island where a white
woman is not absolutely safe anywhere, at any
time or hour. I do not know of a British West Indian island where a white man is in the least danger of being robbed, held up, attacked or insulted.

About the greatest crime that the British West
Indian negro ever commits is petty theft—the
stealing of fruit or produce—and his greatest
racial fault is laziness. But, after all, in lands
where one cannot suffer from the cold, where a

palm-leaf thatch is ample protection from the elements, where food in abundance may be had for the gathering—or by the haphazard cultivation of a few square yards of soil; in such situations, why, I ask, should any man labor? To me it is a never ending source of amazement that the negroes work at all, rather than that they do not toil strenuously and steadily; and it speaks volumes for their ambition and their desire to improve their lot that they do any work whatsoever.

Moreover, the British West Indian negro is not a filthy fellow. By nature he is very cleanly; and, though he may be dressed in the most wretched of rags, he will, if given half a chance, not only bathe his body daily or oftener, but will assiduously wash his rags as well; and in many—I might say most—of the huts of the British West Indian negroes, the floors are far cleaner than the dining tables of the poorer classes of our white laborers.

Moreover, we must bear in mind that in the West Indies there is no color line as we know it. In Jamaica and elsewhere in the British West Indies the question of color—or rather, I might say, a man's classification as belonging to the black, colored or white race—is not so much a matter of ancestry or skin as of education, culture, wealth or influence. Many very light octoroons may be seen laboring side by side with the blackest negroes in the fields or on the roads, and in Jamaica they are deemed and consider themselves as negroes. But on the other hand men of all shades—from the blackest negroes to those who might easily pass for pure whites—may be seen mingling with the white people on equal terms, occupying positions on the judicial bench, holding exalted positions in the Church, politics, medicine, law and commerce. And these consider themselves and are considered by the whites exactly as though they were racially no different. Between these two extremes is the great middle class, composed of individuals of both races and all colors, who are all socially equal and who freely intermarry.

It is largely owing to this entire lack of racial feeling that the colored race predominates and is rapidly increasing in the islands. In the first place, although the infantile mortality is large among the negroes, the race increases more rapidly than the white; in the second place the climate and tropical conditions are far better suited to the colored than to the white race; and in the third place the primitive negro strain is far more virile than the white, and there is a constant tendency for offspring of mixed blood to revert to the African rather than to the Anglo-Saxon type. Even where there is a very small percentage of colored blood— where both parents may be, apparently, pure

[135]

white—the children frequently are decidedly colored or even black. And it is an established biological fact that, should the intermarriage of the two races continue, the result would be, not the absorption of the negro race by the Caucasian, but the annihilation of the Caucasian by the negro, with a wholly colored community as the ultimate result.

To the northerner, with his racial prejudice and his impressions gained through unfortunate experience with the North American negroes, such an intermingling of white and black on terms of social equality may seem very terrible and impossible; but it appears to be admirably suited to the conditions and environment of the West Indies, and is perhaps the best if not the only solution to the problems of such an island as Jamaica. For one thing, it eliminates all danger of race wars or riots; for, with a population consisting of every possible mixture of African and Caucasian blood, it is impossible to draw any hard and fast line between white and black, other than one of education and culture. And there is no question that the colored man is far better fitted to succeed and to survive in the tropics than is the white man.

Moreover, it has been conclusively demonstrated in Jamaica, and elsewhere, that the colored man—or even the negro—if given the same educational and other opportunities as the white, is capable of equaling the latter in intelligence, culture, ability and attainments. Many of the most prominent, the most illustrious, the most highly cultured of West Indians, of both the past and the present, have been men of black or colored blood. Of course these are in a way exceptional cases, but they are exceptional only inasmuch as these men had exceptional advantages. The great majority of the colored population of the island is ignorant and primitive, but so is the great majority of the white races of Europe.

Another point that is far too often overlooked is that we expect too much of the negro. We forget that it has required thousands of years for the white race to attain its present state of advancement, culture and civilization, whereas the negro is but a few generations removed from savagery. And it is preposterous for us to expect that any race can accomplish in one century what another race has accomplished through scores of centuries. The very fact that the negro has so often bridged the gap of thousands of years in a few years is the greatest proof of his natural intelligence and ability.

But, aside from all this, the fact remains that in Jamaica, or elsewhere in the British West Indies, for that matter, an attitude toward the negro is possible and even practical which would be utterly impossible and even dangerous in the north.

Under tropical conditions and environment the West Indian negro has retained far more of the natural primitive traits of his race than has the negro of the United States, who has been bred and reared for generations in a climate and an environment totally foreign to his nature, his psychology and his race. The result has been—quite aside from the difference in the original African stock—that the Jamaican black man is still, by nature, and in mind, character and behavior, more or less the primitive savage, with all the really admirable qualities—as well as many of the faults —of his African ancestors. He is childish rather than vicious; if he commits what civilized man deems a crime, it is, nine times out of ten, done through ignorance, or else because, according to the moral code of primitive man, it is no sin.

Like all savages, he feels that the fruits of the earth were bestowed by God upon mankind for the use and benefit of all, and hence he can see no wrong in helping himself to any fruit, vegetable or natural products. But ninety-nine times out of a hundred he respects another's rights to personal property or the results of another's handiwork— which is also a savage characteristic. Very rarely will he steal money or valuables, and he is un-

[138]

moral rather than immoral. Like the savage, too, he is improvident; he is disinclined to labor unless necessity demands it, and he firmly believes that the chief aim in life is enjoyment rather than toil. He is quite satisfied of the truth of the axiom that sufficient unto the day is the evil thereof, and he is quite content to let the morrow look after itself.

Also, he possesses the savage's love of finery, bright colors, trinkets and gew-gaws; the savage's love of dances and rhythm, and the savage's love for strong drink.

Like most savage, or rather, I might better say, primitive races, he is passionately fond of his home and his family, and yet by nature is more or less of a wanderer. A negro may stick indefinitely to some miserably barren bit of land rather than move from his ancestral home to a better locality; he may be in dire want in some district where he cannot find employment, but prefers to do without rather than transfer himself and family to some place where there is a demand for his services. But, without any apparent reason, he may become a nomad, wandering where his inclination leads; or if he desires some particular thing—usually in the shape of gorgeous raiment—he will go to almost any distance and will labor most strenuously in order to secure it.

And also, like all primitive peoples, he is steeped

[139]

with superstition and, regardless of his professed Christianity and creed, he is at heart a good deal of a pagan, with many of his pagan ancestors' beliefs in good and evil spirits, jumbies, omens and charms, spells and incantations. Also, he possesses the primitive man's generosity, his willingness to share whatever he has with a friend, or even a stranger; he is the soul of hospitality, and, while his gratitude is not deep or lasting, still, once he has formed an attachment for another, he will remain a steadfast friend despite anything and everything.

On the other side of the ledger are the inherent faults—from our point of view—that are common to nearly all primitive races. He is, as I have said, by nature lazy. He allows his animal instincts to rule, rather than to control them. His body is to him of more importance than his mind. He is prone to exaggeration, both in his statements and in his actions, and he has but little conception of the distinction between the truth and a falsehood. He is apt to mistrust a stranger—especially of another race—yet on the other hand he is extremely credulous and gullible and, once his confidence is won, he has implicit faith. He lacks pride in his work or in any accomplishment, and by nature he fairly dotes on litigation of any kind. To the average negro a lawsuit is a most delightful form of amusement, and life would lose half its charm for the negro if he could not haggle and bargain over prices. He is a born arguer and will argue interminably over anything and everything, even though he knows the question never can be settled. Being far less sensitive, mentally and physically, than the white man, he is—to our minds—callous toward his people and his domestic animals. Physical suffering does not affect him as it does us; and, as he does not worry his brain thinking about physical agonies, he suffers far less than we do under the same conditions.

Often he is accused of cowardice, but this is a mistaken idea. The negro—and I am speaking of the Jamaican or West Indian negro as an entity —is as valiant and as courageous as his African forbears when it becomes necessary to be brave. But he may behave like an arrant coward when he feels that there is no reason for risking his life or his skin. And, like most savages, he can work himself into a sort of exalted frenzy—an almost hypnotic state—during which he is absolutely impervious to fear, danger or pain.

Owing to the negro's love of admiration and self-aggrandizement—which also is a universal trait of primitive races—he is ever striving for effect, and has a fine sense of the dramatic, with no mean oratorical powers. And, for much the same reason, he is given to, unconsciously, and quite unintentionally, exaggerating. Often, if a man is hurt a negro will say "Him dead." If a leg or an arm is bruised or injured, the negro will say "Him laig broke." It is not uncommon for him to refer to a train being delayed by stating "the train him fall down." Yet, on the other hand, the negro is most casual when it comes to stating a case exactly. If asked the distance to a certain spot he invariably will reply "Just here" or "Not too far" or "Far enough." Such unimportant matters as dates or spelling receive scant attention. Few negroes can state definitely the dates of their births, and a negro may spell his name a dozen different ways in as many minutes.

He is just as unconcerned over matters which to us would appear most serious and important. He will inform you, with a grin and without the least signs of sorrow, that his father, mother, wife or child is dead; not so much because he does not feel the loss but because, like the child of Nature he is, he regards death as inevitable, a perfectly natural event and little more than a passing incident. Besides, what regret he may feel is more than offset by thoughts of the festivities of the wake, the "front" he will put on by means of an impressive funeral, and the figure he will cut when all dolled out in his mourning clothes.

As a race the West Indian negroes are not artistic. Very few artists, designers, decorators, sculptors or architects have been of colored blood. But on the other hand they are extremely poetical and musical. They sing at their work and they sing at their play. They often express the most beautiful sentiments in a few words, and they can readily improvise music or words of a song to suit any occasion. Their sense of rhythm is amazing, and, as everyone knows, they have a predilection for syncopated music or "jazz" as we call it. Like the old-time deep-sea sailormen, the Jamaican negroes work far better if laboring with a "sing."

The "digging sings" as they are called have a rather peculiar character. They are always led by a man known as the "fugleman," who is the prototype of the old chanteyman and who receives higher wages than the other laborers. The fugleman starts the "sing" by singing a short phrase of the song, and the gang shout the chorus or "bobbin," usually of but one or two words. Each "sing" lasts for only a few minutes—usually three or four—to be followed immediately by a different one. It would seem that the fugleman must possess a most voluminous repertoire to enable him to lead a new song every five minutes, for eight or ten hours; but, as a matter of fact, he usually improvises as he goes along, often taking

some well known song and so altering or garbling
it that it becomes almost or quite unrecognizable.
Very often, too, the "sing" will be an altered form
of some deep-sea chantey, such as "Sally Brown,"
in the West Indian version of which we hear that:

> Sally Brown fall'n th' water,
> Wayee! Sally, Sally Brown.
> Oh, Ah drug she out 'n had n' oughta;
> I'll spen' mah money on Sally Brown.

> Oh, Sally Brown will yo' b'lief me,
> Wayee? Sally, Sally Brown.
> Fo' a 'Badoes nigger she ha' leave me;
> I'll spen' mah money on Sally Brown.

And if we listen to the fugleman we will learn that
our own famous John Brown not only possessed
a donkey, but that the creature was a most amazing freak, for the Jamaicans "sing" has it that:
"John Brown's donkey had a red morocco tail!"

However, neither of these is strictly a "sing,"
although both are used by the negroes when working. Oftentimes they merely hum the air of a
"sing"; and very often the omission of audible
words is quite commendable, as they are more
than spicy. One favorite "sing" is "Mangoose a
come, Dory," which is hummed when the boss or

master appears, and serves as a sort of warning to the gang to work with feverish energy while under his eye. Also, like our own negroes, those of Jamaica are passionately fond of hymns and spirituals, although Moody and Sankey hymns, Salvation Army songs and psalms are the favorites.

In their dances, the Jamaicans formerly used instruments which were the precise counterparts of those used by their ancestors in Africa; but today such are very rarely seen, the drum and the rattle-gourd or sandbox, together with a nutmeg-grater-like affair, rubbed with a stick, being the only savage musical instruments in general use. Of all musical instruments, if it can be classified as such, the drum is the most essential to the negro. Occasionally one may still see the African type of drum —as well as the American Indian and East Indian forms—in use; but as a rule the natives employ the conventional form. In addition to the drum there is usually a flute, fife, piccolo or similar instrument; a banjo or guitar; sometimes a fiddle; a triangle, a rattle-gourd and often, but not always, the roughened scratchy instrument. Be it understood that I am speaking of the orchestras as found in the remote villages and among the country folk, for in the larger towns all the noise and music-making instruments of civilization are in use; and even in distant settlements and huts the ubiquitous gramophone is all too common.

Even in their street cries the Jamaican negroes exhibit their love of music; and, although the old-time cries have largely vanished with the present generation's ultra-modern ideas, as have the picturesque turbans and gaudy cotton-print dresses of the women, still " 'tarch," "peers" mangos and all the other fruits, vegetables and products are always "gwinepas' " (going past) as the buxom negresses swing along with swaying hips and laden trays balanced on woolly heads.

Also, the Jamaican negro has a wealth of proverbs. Some of these are undoubtedly of African origin, but the majority have been borrowed—in almost unrecognizable form—from those in use by Europeans everywhere.

Among the latter may be mentioned the following: "Too-much-hurry get dey tomorry, tek-time get dey today." "Greedy choke puppy." "Rock-'tone a ribber bottom never know sun hot." "When yo' play wif puppy, puppy lick yo' mouf." "Darg hab lib'ty fe watch gubnor." "Cuss-cuss neber bore hole in a me 'kin." "Ebery man know wha' him own house leak." "No eberyting wha' got sugar a sweet." "Coward man keep soun' bone." "Big words break nobody's 'kin." "Cashew never bear guava."

Ocho Rios, near St. Ann's Bay, a pretty scene on a glorious coast road

Courtesy of George Pearson, Kingston

Wag Water River

Of the proverbs of African origin we have: "When fish come out o' sea an' tell yo' alligator hab fever, belieb he." "One daddy fe twenty picknie, but twenty picknie no fe one daddy." "One finger can't catch louse." "If snake bite yo', yo' see lizard you run."

In folklore the Jamaican negroes are rather poor. Even the Anancy stories are gradually dying out. These are in reality African folklore adapted to Jamaican conditions, and are of three types. First, those dealing with a mythical personage named Anancy, together with his wife, Crooky, and his son, Tocooma; second, the stories dealing with an old witch; and third, a number of stories in which man and inanimate objects are the characters.

Neither are the Jamaicans so given to jumbies and jumbie tales as are the colored folk of the other British islands. Of course they believe in their jumbies—what country negro in the West Indies does not?—but their ideas of these strange African spirits or specters are somewhat vague, and they have none of the intricate, involved and extremely comprehensive jumbie lore that is so common, I might say universal, in the islands where the people are of mixed French and African blood. In those islands jumbies and jumbie tales predominate, and supernatural occurrences—according to the negroes—are very common. But reported "showers of stones"—which by the way actually *do* occur and have been vouched for by the most hard-headed, intelligent and veracious white men, though never explained—are about the only supernatural occurrences that take place in Jamaica.

As I have already said, the Jamaican negroes are not naturally vicious nor even disorderly. On the contrary, they are extremely orderly. They have the true British regard and respect for laws, and they are usually quite willing to take the punishment meted out to them for violation of the law, without grumbling. But the negro is quick to see when an injustice is done and quick to resent it. Also, he fears and hates ridicule more than scolding, cursing or even a beating. He is a cheerful optimist, and even when drunk—and the negro is not usually a drunkard—he rarely becomes quarrelsome or abusive. Neither is the Jamaican negro, when placed in authority or decked in a uniform, the overbearing, self-important creature that his northern kinsman becomes under similar conditions. The black drivers and conductors of tramcars, busses, etc., are the most respectful, polite and courteous of men, and are particularly noticeable for their kindness, patience and real solicitude when dealing with children, elderly people or the infirm. The black "bobbies" are ever respectful and quiet and possess unlimited patience, while the uniformed attendants in the largest hotels, in government buildings, etc., are invariably courteous and polite. It is perhaps in this universal deference and respect which the Jamaica exhibits toward his superiors—whether white or colored—that he differs the most from our northern negro.

And this respectful attitude was even more marked before the World War. Unfortunately, the West Indian colored troops acquired some mighty bad habits when overseas, and returned to Jamaica completely altered in their outlook on life and their behavior. To be sure, their experience had one good result: they acquired a taste for conditions, money and life which they could not satisfy without bucking up and putting their noses to the grindstone. But along with this they learned of unions, strikes, communism and a lot of other undesirable matters. Even burglary began to make itself noticeable in and about Kingston. This was unprecedented, the worst pilfering of the negroes before then having consisted of the most petty thefts. Indeed, so universally honest were the negroes that, after the destruction of Kingston in 1907, when houses, shops and even banks were left gaping with fortunes in money, jewels and valuables—not to mention food, clothing and personal effects—exposed, practically no thefts were reported, although scores of negroes roamed about at will and might easily have helped themselves to anything they desired.

Another difference between the Jamaican and the North American negro is that of language, or perhaps better, dialect. The average (I am speaking of the uneducated, working or peasant class) Jamaican is not at all the loquacious being that we know in the north or that is so typical of Barbados, Demerara and many other British colonies. He is, in fact, rather inarticulate, and is far more like his African ancestor in his use of gestures in place of words to express his ideas and feelings. And what language he does use is a strange jargon totally distinct from the northern negro's dialect, wholly different from the dialect of any other West Indian island, and so unlike the negroid Cockney of the larger towns that a country negro finds it almost as difficult to converse intelligently with his city fellow as with a stranger from overseas. Not only is his vocabulary very limited; he clips his words, omits letters, does away entirely with articles, confuses genders and persons and gives no heed to verbs. It is so clearly defined as a distinct dialect that the white planters employ it in addressing the negroes, just as the whites address the Chinese coolies in "Pidgin English" in China, or use "Talky-talky" in Guiana.

Another peculiarity of the negro—which on more than one occasion has struck terror to the hearts of female tourists from the north—is his habit of talking to himself as he walks along the road or goes about his work. But this does not—as the uninitiated sometimes assume—signify that the fellow is drunk or crazy. He merely is thinking aloud, soliloquizing, talking matters over with himself; and, curiously enough, at such times he frequently assumes a dual personality, the one conversing and arguing with the other quite as seriously and as earnestly as though two really separate individuals.

Taken all in all, the Jamaican colored folk are a rather likable lot, and to the person interested in his fellow men and in human nature they form one of the most interesting features of the island. But it is almost hopeless for the white man really to understand the negro, to get "under his skin" so to speak. Only by long association with negroes of all types and classes, by dwelling among them, employing them, listening to them, taking part in their joys and sorrows, listening to and—apparently at least—accepting their weird tales and strange beliefs; only by casting aside all racial prejudices and judging the negroes by their personalities rather than their color; by meeting and mingling on equal terms with those of the educated, cultured class, can any white man even begin to understand the negro's psychology, his character and his mentality. I have done all this and more. For over thirty years I have dealt more or less continuously with the West Indian negroes. Some of them I number among my best and most esteemed friends. I have had negro camp-boys as my sole companions for months at a time in the bush. I have dwelt in the most remote mountain villages and the most isolated negro huts, and yet I still feel very much as did the Jamaican planter who said: "When I had been here twenty years I thought I understood the negroes. Now that I have been here over thirty years I am sure I don't understand them at all!"

CHAPTER IX

AUTOMOBILE TOURS

If touring in a hired car, it is more satisfactory to arrange for the automobile on a mileage basis, unless a comparatively short trip is planned, with an hour or more waiting time—as for example a visit to Castleton Gardens—when arrangements should be made as to charges for waiting time.

There is no fixed rate for hired cars in Jamaica, but the best cars may be had at from 9d (18c.) to 1s 6d. (36c.) a mile, according to size of car. When a single run from one place to another is made—as from Kingston to Port Antonio—the person hiring the car is expected to defray the cost of the return journey. This should be arranged in advance.

If the projected tour is to be of more than one day, the chauffeur's expenses are usually extra, unless otherwise arranged in advance. These are reckoned at 8s. ($2.00) per day, which includes food and lodging. Accommodations for chauffeurs are arranged by themselves. All the livery chauffeurs are familiar with all parts of the island. If desired, the hire of cars and all arrangements for

[153]

tours may be made through the Tourist Bureau, free of charge for services.

Motor cars can be hired for from 6d. (12c.) up to 1s. 6d. (36c.) per mile.

The cost of hiring an automobile varies according to the type of car, mileage per day, length of trip, etc.

For example, the 7-day Tour (No. 27), outlined on page 159, provides for an average of about 75 miles a day (motor car owners usually stipulate an average minimum run of about 50 miles a day), and the cost would work out as follows:—

524 miles reckoned at 9d. (18c.) per mile	£19	13	0	($98.25)
Chauffeur's expenses: 7 days at 8/- ($2) per day	2	16	0	($14.00)
Total	£22	9	0	($112.25)

If three persons are touring together it will be seen that the cost of the car for the above trip, for each person, would be:— £7 9 8 ($37.42)

Hotels might be reckoned at an average of £1 ($5) per day, for 7 days	£7	0	0	($35.00)
Cost of 7-day Automobile Tour (if 3 travel together), each person ..	£14	9	8	($72.42)

JAMAICA OF TODAY

If accommodation is taken at smaller hotels, boarding-houses or private houses, the cost of accommodation as above can be practically halved.

AUTOMOBILE TOURS IN JAMAICA

HALF-DAY TRIPS FROM KINGSTON

	Miles
1. Spanish Town and Bog Walk	50
2. Spanish Town and Bog Walk, returning via Glengoffe, Lawrence Tavern and Stony Hill .	60
3. This trip can be extended by going on from Bog Walk to Riversdale (Natural Bridge) prior to returning via Glengoffe, etc. (adding about 10 miles to the trip)	70
4. Newcastle (Military cantonment in Port Royal mountains) and Hardwar Gap (4,079 feet)	44
5. Castleton Botanic Gardens, via Constant Spring and Stony Hill	39
6. Cane River Falls and Bathing Place, via Rockfort	21
7. Gordon Town, Guava Ridge, Mavis Bank (starting point for climbing Blue Mountain Peak)	34

ONE-DAY TRIPS FROM KINGSTON

8. Newcastle, Hardwar Gap, Buff Bay and return via Annotto Bay, Castleton Botanic Gardens and Stony Hill (lunch * at Hardwar Gap) ..	84
9. Rockfort, Yallahs Bay, Rozelle, Morant Bay, Trinity Ville, Cedar Valley, Llandewey, Albion, Rockfort (lunch * at Morant Bay)	81
10. Stony Hill, Castleton Botanic Gardens, Law-	

Miles

rence Tavern, Glengoffe, Bog Walk, Spanish
Town (lunch * at Castleton) 70

11. Rockfort, Morant Bay, Port Morant, Bath
(Mineral Springs) and return via Morant
Bay, Trinity Ville, Cedar Valley, etc. (lunch *
at Bath) 95

12. Port Antonio via Castleton Botanic Gardens
and return via Manchioneal, Port Morant,
etc. (lunch at Port Antonio) 144

13. Port Antonio via Newcastle and Hardwar Gap
and return via Castleton Gardens (lunch at
Port Antonio) 122

14. Moneague, via Spanish Town, Bog Walk and
Mount Diablo, returning same way (lunch at
Moneague Hotel) 86

15. Mandeville via Spanish Town, returning same
way (lunch at Mandeville) 122

16. St. Ann's Bay, via Moneague, Fern Gully, Ocho
Rios, Dunn's River Bathing Beach, Roaring
River Falls, and return via Claremont and
Moneague (lunch at Osborne Hotel, St. Ann's
Bay) 125

TWO-DAY TOURS FROM KINGSTON

17. 1st Day.—Kingston—Mandeville (lunch) 60
miles, Cave Valley, Brown's Town, St. Ann's
Bay, (dine and sleep at Osborne Hotel) 56
miles.

2nd Day.—Roaring River Falls, Dunn's River
Falls and Bathing Beach, Ocho Rios, Fern
Gully, Moneague (lunch at Moneague Hotel),

[156]

Miles

Mount Diablo, Bog Walk, Spanish Town,
Kingston, 61 177

18. 1st Day.—Kingston—Port Antonio (via coastal
road and east end of island), 82 miles.
2nd Day.—Port Antonio, Kingston (via Castleton Botanic Gardens), 62 144

19. 1st Day.—Kingston—Newcastle, Buff Bay, Port
Maria, 62 miles.
2nd Day.—Port Maria, Ocho Rios, Fern Gully,
Moneague, Kingston, 74 136

20. 1st Day.—Kingston—St. Ann's Bay, Montego
Bay, 130 miles.
2nd Day.—Montego Bay (via New Market and
Lacovia) to Mandeville, Kingston, 131 261

THREE-DAY TOURS FROM KINGSTON

Miles Miles

21. 1st Day.—Kingston—Port Antonio (via
Bath). (Via Castleton Gardens, 20
miles less) 82
2nd Day.—Port Antonio—St. Ann's Bay 71
3rd Day.—St. Ann's Bay—Kingston 61
——— 214

22. 1st Day.—Kingston—Buff Bay (via Newcastle), Port Maria 64
2nd Day.—Port Maria, St. Ann's Bay,
Mandeville 83
3rd Day.—Mandeville—Kingston 61
——— 208

23. 1st Day.—Kingston—St. Ann's Bay 61
2nd Day.—St. Ann's Bay—Montego Bay 69

[157]

Miles Miles

3rd Day.—Montego Bay, Mandeville, Kingston 131

— 261

FOUR-DAY TOUR FROM KINGSTON

24. 1st Day.—Kingston—Port Antonio (via Bath). (Via Castleton Gardens, 20 miles less) 82

2nd Day.—Port Antonio—St. Ann's Bay —St. Ann's Bay—Montego Bay 140

3rd Day.—Montego Bay—Mandeville (via Black River) 91

4th Day.—Mandeville—Kingston 61

— 374

FIVE-DAY TOUR FROM KINGSTON

25. 1st Day.—Kingston—Port Antonio (via Newcastle) 61

2nd Day.—Port Antonio—Moneague (via Ocho Rios) 76

3rd Day.—Moneague—Mandeville 68

4th Day.—Mandeville—Montego Bay (via Black River) 91

5th Day.—Montego Bay—Kingston (via St. Ann's Bay) 130

— 426

SIX-DAY TOUR FROM KINGSTON

26. 1st Day.—Kingston—Port Antonio (via Bath). (Via Castleton Gardens, 20 miles less) 82

Miles Miles

2nd Day.—Port Antonio—Moneague (via
Hardwar Gap, Halfway Tree, Spanish
Town) 100

3rd Day.—Moneague—Mandeville 68

4th Day.—Mandeville—Montego Bay (via
Black River) 91

5th Day.—Montego Bay—St. Ann's Bay 69

6th Day.—St. Ann's Bay—Kingston (via
Port Maria and Castleton Botanic Gardens) 74
—— 484

SEVEN-DAY TOUR FROM KINGSTON

27. 1st Day.—Kingston—Port Antonio (via
Bath). (Via Castleton Gardens, 20
miles less) 82

2nd Day.—Port Antonio—Moneague (via
Castleton, Glengoffe, Bog Walk) 82

3rd Day.—Moneague—Mandeville 68

4th Day.—Mandeville—Montego Bay (via
Black River) 91

5th Day.—Montego Bay—St. Ann's Bay 69

6th Day.—St. Ann's Bay—Port Antonio . 71

7th Day.—Port Antonio—Kingston (via
Newcastle) 61
—— 524

FOURTEEN-DAY TOUR FROM KINGSTON

28. 1st Day.—Kingston—Mandeville (via
Vere and Milk River Baths) 78

[159]

Miles Miles

2nd Day.—Mandeville (Excursions, etc., in neighborhood)

3rd Day.—Mandeville—Malvern 29

4th Day.—Malvern—Montego Bay 58

5th Day.—Montego Bay

6th Day.—Montego Bay—St. Ann's Bay 69

7th Day.—St. Ann's Bay—Mandeville .. 56

8th Day.—Mandeville, Spanish Town, Moneague 77

9th Day.—Moneague

10th Day.—Moneague, Ocho Rios, Port Maria, Castleton, Halfway Tree, Hardwar Gap 87

11th Day.—Hardwar Gap

12th Day.—Hardwar Gap—Port Antonio 40

13th Day.—Port Antonio

14th Day.—Port Antonio—Kingston (via Bath) 82

—— 576

Mileage of trips during stay in towns, etc., say .. 124

—— 700

——

* Take lunch-basket in car.

DAY AND HALF AUTOMOBILE TOURS

Ret.

Moneague, via Spanish Town, Bog Walk and Mount Diablo, returning by the same route 86

Mandeville via Spanish Town, returning by same route 122

JAMAICA OF TODAY

	Miles
St. Ann's Bay via Moneague, Fern Gully, Ocho Rios, Dunn's River Bathing Beach, Roaring River Falls, returning via Claremont and Moneague	125
Gordon Town, Guava Ridge, Mavis Bank (starting point for climbing Blue Mountain Peak)	34
Newcastle, Hardwar Gap, Buff Bay, Annotto Bay, Castleton Botanical Gardens, Stony Hill, Constant Spring, Kingston	84
Rockfort, Yallahs Bay, Rozelle, Morant Bay, Trinity Ville, Cedar Valley, Llandewey, Rockfort	81
Bath (Thermal Spring) and Botanical Gardens	90
Rockfort, Morant Bay, Port Morant, Bath (Mineral Spring) and return via Morant Bay, Trinity Ville, Cedar Valley, etc.	95
Port Antonio, via Castleton Botanic Gardens, and return via Manchioneal, Port Morant, etc.	144
Port Antonio via Newcastle and Hardwar Gap and return via Castleton Gardens	122
Spanish Town (former Capital of Jamaica), Old Cathedral, Government Buildings, Rodney Memorial, etc.	27
Spanish Town and Bog Walk, a beautiful scenic run	50

(The above trips can also be done by Railway.)

Spanish Town and Bog Walk, returning via Glengoffe, Lawrence Tavern and Stony Hill	60
Stony Hill, Castleton Botanical Gardens, Lawrence Tavern, Glengoffe, Bog Walk, Spanish Town	70
Newcastle (Military Cantonment), elevation 3,719 feet, and Hardwar Gap, 4,079 feet	44
Cane River Falls and Bathing Place, via Rockfort	21

COMBINED AUTOMOBILE AND RAILWAY CIRCULAR TOURS

(From one to four days)

BY RAILWAY	AUTO	RAILWAY
Kingston–Frankfield.	Frankfield–Mandeville–Williamsfield.	Williamsfield–Kingston.
"	Frankfield–Ulster Spring–Falmouth–Montego Bay.	Montego Bay–Kingston.
Montego Bay.	Montego Bay–Port Antonio.	Port Antonio–Kingston.
Ipswich or Maggotty.	Ipswich or Maggotty–Black River or Malvern, Mandeville–Williamsfield.	Williamsfield–Kingston.
Ewarton.	Ewarton–Montego Bay.	Montego Bay–Kingston.
"	Ewarton–Port Antonio.	Port Antonio–Kingston.
"	Ewarton–St. Ann's Bay–Frankfield.	Frankfield–Kingston.
"	Ewarton–Castleton Gardens–Kingston.	
Williamsfield.	Williamsfield–Mandeville–Christiana–Cave Valley–St. Ann's Bay–Annotto Bay.	Annotto Bay–Kingston.
Balaclava.	Balaclava–Black River–Savanna-la-Mar–Lucea–Montego Bay.	Montego Bay–Kingston.
"	Balaclava–Black River–Malvern–Williamsfield.	Williamsfield–Kingston.
Williamsfield.	Williamsfield–Christiana–Falmouth–Ulster Spring–Montego Bay.	Montego Bay–Kingston.
Clarendon Park.	Clarendon Park–Milk River Baths–Vere–Old Harbour.	Old Harbour–Kingston.
Port Antonio.	Port Antonio–New Castle–Kingston.	

The countryside in Jamaica, near Kent Village, Bog Walk

JAMAICA OF TODAY

A Picturesque Route Through Old-World Jamaica

From Kingston to:—

Spanish town	13	miles
Old Harbour	25	"
Rock River	41	"
Frankfield	59	"
Spaldings	69	"
Mandeville (Via Spaldings)	81	"
Brown's Town "	97	"
Falmouth "	121	"
Montego Bay "	143	"

To those who conceive the idea that because Jamaica is a small island, there cannot be very much to see in it, the assurance can be given that it is possible for one to stay in the island for twelve months without seeing every place and object of interest. How many tourists, for instance, have traversed that delightful, picturesque route from the little town of Old Harbour on into Upper Clarendon and thence to Mandeville or to other places as outlined above?

Turning to the right or northward from Old Harbour, one passes in succession, Bodle's Pen, Colbeck Castle, Seven's Plantation, Longville, Moore's, Retreat Copper Mines, to the village of Rock River and over the Old Spanish Bridge, through Low Ground, Sutton's, Chapelton, Danks

[163]

and Savoy Sugar plantations, Morgan's Valley, Trout Hall, Frankfield to Spaldings. At Spaldings routes branch off to Mandeville, etc.

Not only beautiful and picturesque scenery is enjoyed, but an historic atmosphere reminiscent of the days when British forces took possession of Jamaica from the Spaniards. Colbeck Castle, early on the run, is the only genuine moat-surrounded fortress on the island, and the ruins are in a fair state of preservation.

The plantations mentioned, such as "Sevens," "Longville," etc., were settled by notabilities, in some cases 250 years or more ago. For instance, Samuel Long, of Longville, came with the British Conquerors—Penn and Venables—in 1655. On the banks of the Rio Minho—which flows through the property—he found basins where the Indians and the Spaniards washed gold.

The interest of tourists is arrested at various points—sugar works are to be seen, copper mines, some fine arches of old Spanish bridge-work, and a variety of agricultural activities.

Near "Retreat," Bull Head Mountain comes into view. This elevation is the highest point in this particular mountain range and marks practically the center of the island.

A specially-written pamphlet, which can be obtained free from the Tourist Bureau, Kingston, contains a pictorial description of this most interesting route.

JAMAICA OF TODAY

Jamaica is very accessible by steamships from almost any portion of the world; and, in addition to the regular lines plying between the island and other ports, there are many cruise ships which make Jamaica a place of call during the winter season.

FROM THE UNITED STATES: Three regular lines sail for Jamaica. These are:

THE UNITED FRUIT COMPANY, from New York, Boston, New Orleans.

DI GIORGIO FRUIT COMPANY, from New York.

ATLANTIC FRUIT COMPANY, from New York, Philadelphia and Baltimore.

FROM CANADA:

CANADIAN NATIONAL STEAMSHIPS, between Jamaica and Montreal from May until November and between Kingston and Halifax during the winter months.

FROM GREAT BRITAIN:

ELDERS AND FYFFES LTD., Regular sailings from England (Avonmouth and Liverpool) to Jamaica, and other British West Indies.

JAMAICA DIRECT FRUIT LINE LTD., between London and Jamaica.

FROM EUROPE:

HORN LINE. To and from Hamburg and Jamaica. Also to Le Havre.

ELDERS AND FYFFES LTD. From Rotterdam.

[165]

FARES, ETC., FROM CITY TO PLACES IN AND NEAR CITY

	Miles from City	FARES (Each Person)	
		Tram-car (from City) to nearest point	Taxi-cabs and Horse "Busses"
TOURIST BUREAU (87, BARRY STREET)	City	2d. (4c.)	6d. (12c.)
Hotels:—			
Myrtle Bank (Harbour Street)	½	2d.	6d.
South Camp Road Hotel (South Camp Road)	1	2d.	6d.
Earl's Court Hotel (18, North Street)	¾	2d.	6d.
Melrose House Hotel (117, Duke Street)	¾	2d.	9d.
The Doric Hotel (94, East Street)	¾	2d.	6d.
The Grenville Hotel (112, East Street)	¾	2d.	6d.
Roslyn Hall—Guest House—Matilda's Corner, Old			
Hope Rd.)	4	4d. (8c.)	9/6 (87c.)
Mona Great House Hotel (Liguanea, St. Andrew)	5	4d.	5/- ($1.25)
Manor House Hotel (Constant Spring)	6	4d.	5/- ($1.25)
General Post Office and Telegraph Office (King Street)	City	2d.	6d.
Public Buildings and Government Offices (King Street)	"	2d.	6d.
Kingston and St. Andrew Corporation and Town Clerk			
(Church Street)	..	2d.	6d.
Legislative Council Chamber (Duke Street)	..	2d.	6d.
Cable Offices:—			
The Direct West India Cable Co., Ltd., (8, Port Royal			
Street)	"	2d.	6d.
The West India and Panama Telegraph Co., Ltd. (8,			
Port Royal Street)	"	2d.	6d.
Jamaica Chamber of Commerce and Merchant's Ex-			
change (King Street)	..	2d.	6d.
The Jamaica Imperial Association (85–87, Barry Street)	..	2d.	6d.
Jamaica Agriculture Society (North Parade)	..	2d.	6d.
American Consulate (Church Street)	..	2d.	6d.
Institute of Jamaica Library and Museum (East Street)	..	2d.	6d.
Kingston Atheneum Literary Society (Harbour Street)	..	2d.	6d.
Victoria Market (King Street)	..	2d.	6d.

	Miles		
Jubilee (or "Sollas") Market, (Orange Street)	"	2d. (8c.)	6d. (62c.) *
King's House Gate	4	4d.	2/6 ($1.25) *
Hope (Government) Botanical Gardens	4	4d.	5/- *
Hope (Government) Farm School	5	4d.	5/- *
Papine (Tram Terminus)	6	4d.	5/- *
Constant Spring, Golf Club (Tram Terminus)	6	4d.	5/- *
Rockfort Gardens (Tram Terminus)	3	2d.	3/6 (87c.) *
Bournemouth Bath	2½	2d.	1/6 (37c.) *
Royal Jamaica Yacht Club	1	2d.	9d. (18c.) *
Liguanea Club and Golf Course	2½	2d.	2/- (50c.) *
St. Andrew's Club	1¾	4d.	1/6 *
The Jamaica Club	½	2d.	6d.
Y. M. C. A. (Hanover Street)	½	2d.	6d.
Y. W. C. A. (North Street)	½	2d.	6d.
Masonic Temple (80 Hanover Street)	¾	2d.	6d.
"Palace," Picture Theatre	½	2d.	6d.
"Gaiety," Picture Theatre	¼	2d.	1/6 *
"Movies," Cross Roads		2d.	1/6 *
Up Park Camp (South Camp Road)	2	2d.	9d.
Kingston Race Course (East Street)	2	2d.	6d.
Railway Station	1	2d.	
	City		

* These journeys are not covered by Regulations and the fares must be arranged between passenger and driver before starting. The fares shown are the minimum for one person.

Taxi-cabs are distinguished by a white band about two inches in width round the body of the car.

FARES BY TIME.

Between the hours of 6 A. M. and 10 P. M.:—

	Taxi-cabs.	Horse drawn "cabs."
For any time within and not exceeding half an hour	4/- ($1.00)	2/- (50c.)
For any time above half an hour and not exceeding one hour	10/- ($2.50)	5/- ($1.25)
For every additional half an hour or part of half an hour after the first hour	4/- ($1.00)	2/- (50c.)

Between the hours of 10 P. M. and 6 A. M. the above rates are increased 50 per cent.

The above rates apply only to the Corporate Areas of Kingston and St. Andrew.

The limits of these areas are, viz.:—

Hope Road.
Constant Spring Road.
Spanish Town Road.
Rockfort Road.

Matilda's Corner.
Halfway Tree Clock.
Greenwich Street.
Elletson Road.

If vehicles are engaged for trips beyond and outside areas given, terms should be arranged with the drivers before the journey is commenced, but generally speaking taxi-cabs can be hired at 6d. per mile. (12c. per mile).

RAILWAY TIME TABLE

KINGSTON-MONTEGO BAY SECTION

Kingston → Montego Bay (reading down)

Station	Fares from Kingston 1st s. d.	2nd s. d.	Daily Except Sundays a.m.	a.m.	p.m.
Kingston ....dep	—	—	7.25	10.45	4.15
Gregory Park	1 0	0 6	7.42	11.05	4.32
Grange Lane	1 6	0 9	7.50	11.13	4.40
Spanish Town	2 0	1 0	8.03	11.25	4.51
Hartlands	2 8	1 4	8.15	11.35	5.02
Bushy Park	3 8	1 10	8.27	11.47	5.14
Old Harbour	4 4	2 2	8.38	11.58	5.25
			a.m.	p.m.	p.m.
May Pen	6 2	3 1	9.09	12.28	5.56
Four Paths	6 4	3 2	9.21	12.40	6.08
Clarendon Park	8 6	4 3	9.40	1.00	6.26
Williamsfield	9 8	4 8	10.10	1.13	6.39
Kendal	10 0	5 0	10.52	1.44	7.15
Greenvale	10 2	5 1	11.00	1.55	7.23
Balaclava	12 4	6 2	—	2.20	Wednes days only
Appleton	14 2	7 1	—	3.03	
Maggotty	15 2	7 7	—	3.27	
Ipswich	16 2	8 1	—	3.38	a.m.
Stonehenge Siding	19 2	9 7	—	4.06	8.15
Catadupa	19 2	9 7	—	4.28	8.40
Cambridge	19 2	9 7	—	4.42	9.02
Montpelier	20 0	10 0	—	5.00	9.15
Anchovy	21 0	10 6	—	5.25	9.40
Montego Bay ..(arr)	23 0	11 6	—	5.38	—
				6.00	

Montego Bay → Kingston (reading down)

Station	Fares from Montego Bay 1st s. d.	2nd s. d.	Daily except Sundays a.m.	a.m.	p.m.	Wed.'s only p.m.
Montego Bay ....dep	—	—	—	7.30	—	4.30
Anchovy	1 6	0 9	—	7.56	—	4.58
Montpelier	2 2	1 1	—	8.13	—	5.20
Cambridge	3 2	1 7	—	8.34	—	5.44
Catadupa	4 0	2 0	—	8.54	—	6.00
Stonehenge Siding	4 8	2 4	—	9.06	—	
Ipswich	5 8	2 10	—	9.26	—	
Maggotty	6 10	3 5	—	9.49	—	
Appleton	7 6	3 9	—	10.05	—	
Balaclava	8 10	4 5	—	10.37	—	
Greenvale	10 2	5 1	—	11.24	—	
Kendal ......dep	12 2	6 1	6.00	11.51	2.00	
			a.m.	p.m.	p.m.	
Williamsfield	12 6	6 3	6.12	12.09	2.20	
Porus	13 10	6 11	6.37	12.37	3.20	
Clarendon Park	14 8	7 4	6.53	12.54	3.36	
Four Paths	15 10	7 11	7.07	1.08	3.50	
May Pen	16 2	8 1	7.25	1.26	4.11	
Old Harbour	18 10	8 9	7.52	1.55	4.39	
Bushy Park	19 4	9 5	8.00	2.03	4.47	
Hartlands	20 6	9 8	8.12	2.16	5.03	
Spanish Town	21 6	10 3	8.35	2.41	5.22	
Grange Lane	21 6	10 9	8.44	2.50	5.31	
Kingston Park ...arr	23 0	11 6	9.00	3.05	5.39	
					9.55	

KINGSTON-MAY PEN-FRANKFIELD SECTION

Kingston → Frankfield (reading down)

Station	Fares from Kingston 1st s. d.	2nd s. d.	Daily except Sundays a.m.	p.m.
Kingston ....dep	—	—	7.25	4.15
Gregory Park	1 0	0 6	7.42	4.32
Grange Lane	1 6	0 9	7.50	4.40
Spanish Town	2 0	1 0	8.03	4.51
Hartlands	2 8	1 4	8.15	5.02
Bushy Park	3 8	1 10	8.27	5.14
Old Harbour	4 4	2 2	8.38	5.25
May Pen	6 2	3 1	9.15	6.00
Suttons	8 2	4 1	10.00	6.45
Chapelton	9 2	4 7	10.25	7.08
Morgan's Pass	10 4	5 2	10.39	7.22
Crooked River	10 6	5 3	10.54	7.39
Trout Hall			11.04	7.49

Frankfield → Kingston (reading down)

Station	Fares from Frankfield 1st s. d.	2nd s. d.	Daily except Sundays a.m.	p.m.
Frankfield ....dep	—	—	5.15	2.05
Trout Hall	1 0	0 6	5.27	2.20
Crooked River	2 2	0 11	5.35	2.28
Morgans Pass	2 2	1 1	5.49	2.42
Chapelton	3 0	1 6	6.06	3.10
Suttons	5 0	3 3	6.26	3.30
May Pen	6 10	4 3	7.25	4.11
Old Harbour	7 6	4 7	7.52	4.39
Bushy Park	8 2	4 8	8.00	4.47
Hartlands	9 8	4 10	8.12	5.03
Spanish Town	10 0	5 0	8.26	5.22
Grange Lane			8.35	5.31
Gregory Park			8.44	5.39

KINGSTON–PORT ANTONIO SECTION

Station	Fares from Kingston 1st s. d.	2nd s. d.	Daily except Sunday p.m.	Sundays only a.m.	Sundays only p.m.	Sats. only a.m.
Kingston ...... dep.	1 0	0 6	2.15	7.15	2.20	—
Gregory Park	1 6	0 9	2.32	7.32	2.37	—
Grange Lane	2 0	0 9	2.42	7.42	2.47	—
Spanish Town	3 10	1 11	2.54	7.54	2.59	—
Bog Walk	5 0	2 7	3.22	8.22	3.27	—
Riversdale	6 0	3 0	3.39	8.39	3.44	—
Troja	7 6	3 6	3.57	8.58	4.02	—
Richmond	7 6	3 6	4.20	9.20	4.25	—
Highgate	8 0	4 3	4.30	9.30	4.32	—
Albany	10 0	5 0	4.47	9.47	4.55	—
Belfield Siding	11 10	5 11	4.58	9.58	5.03	—
Annotto Bay	10 0	5 0	5.13	10.13	5.18	8.36
Windsor Castle	11 10	5 11	5.27	10.27	5.32	8.47
Buff Bay	13 6	6 3	5.40	10.40	5.45	9.04
Orange Bay	13 2	6 9	5.50	10.50	5.55	—
Hope Bay	14 2	7 1	6.05	11.05	6.10	9.16
St. Margaret's Bay	15 2	7 7	6.16	11.16	6.21	9.35
Port Antonio ... arr.			6.35	11.35	6.40	—

Station	Fares from Port Antonio 1st s. d.	2nd s. d.	Daily except Sunday a.m.	Sundays only a.m.	Sundays only p.m.	Saturdays only p.m.
Port Antonio ... dep.			7.00	6.15	2.00	4.20
St. Margaret's Bay	1 4	0 8	7.19	6.34	2.19	4.41
Hope Bay	1 10	0 11	7.29	6.44	2.29	4.53
Orange Bay	3 6	1 9	7.44	7.10	2.44	5.10
Buff Bay	4 4	2 2	7.55	7.22	2.55	5.19
Windsor Castle	5 2	2 7	8.07	7.37	3.07	—
Annotto Bay	6 10	3 5	8.22	7.51	3.22	—
Belfield Siding	6 10	3 5	8.36	8.03	3.36	—
Albany	7 8	3 10	8.48	8.22	3.48	—
Highgate	8 2	4 1	9.07	8.36	4.07	—
Richmond	8 2	4 7	9.21	8.57	4.21	—
Troja	9 2	4 7	9.42	9.14	4.42	—
Riversdale	10 6	5 9	9.59	9.34	4.59	—
Bog Walk	11 6	5 9	10.19	10.01	5.19	—
Spanish Town	13 8	6 10	10.46	10.11	5.46	—
Grange Lane	13 8	6 10	10.56	10.19	5.56	—
Gregory Park	14 0	7 0	11.04	10.19	6.04	—
Kingston ...... arr.	15 2	7 7	11.20	10.35	6.20	—

KINGSTON–EWARTON SECTION.

Station	Fares from Kingston 1st s. d.	2nd s. d.	Daily except Sundays a.m.	Daily except Sundays p.m.
Kingston ...... dep.	1 0	0 6	7.25	2.15
Gregory Park	1 6	0 9	7.42	2.32
Grange Lane	2 0	0 9	7.50	2.42
Spanish Town	3 10	1 11	8.30	2.54
Bog Walk	4 6	2 3	8.58	3.26
Linstead	4 6	2 3	9.10	3.39
Ewarton ...... arr.	5 6	2 9	9.25	3.53

Station	Fares from Ewarton 1st s. d.	2nd s. d.	Daily Except Sundays a.m.	Daily Except Sundays p.m.
Ewarton ...... dep.	1 0	0 6	9.46	4.15
Linstead	1 10	0 11	10.04	4.33
Bog Walk	3 6	1 9	10.19	4.48
Spanish Town	4 4	2 2	10.46	5.22
Grange Lane	4 4	2 2	10.56	5.31
Gregory Park	5 6	2 9	11.04	5.39
Kingston ...... arr.			11.20	5.55

NOTE:—
(1) First Class Return Tickets are issued at Single Fare-and-a-half available for 14 days.
(2) Week End Second Class Return Tickets are issued at Single Fare-and-a-half on Fridays and Saturdays, available to return on Sundays or Mondays.
(3) Return Tickets are issued for the Sunday Trains available for day of issue only at Single Fare-and-a-half.
The Director of the Jamaica Government Railway is Mr. John Powter, C.B.E.

FROM CUBA:

UNITED FRUIT COMPANY, from Havana and Santiago de Cuba.

ATLANTIC FRUIT LINE, from Havana.

FROM WEST INDIES:

ELDERS & FYFFES LTD., to and from Barbados, Trinidad, Bermuda.

CANADIAN NATIONAL STEAMSHIPS, calling at Bermuda and Nassau.

HORN LINE, stops at San Juan, Porto Rico. Porto Plata, Santo Domingo. Cape Haitien, Port au Prince. San Pedro de Macoris, Santo Domingo. Santo Domingo City. Jacmel, Aux Cayes. Curaçao. Trinidad.

CAYMAN ISLANDS SERVICE:

CAYMAN ISLANDS MOTOR BOAT CO. LTD.

SOUTH AND CENTRAL AMERICA:

UNITED FRUIT COMPANY. Stops at Costa Rica, Honduras, Panama.

HORN LINE. Calls at La Guaira, Venezuela. Porto Cabello, Venezuela. Santa Marta, Porto Colombia and Cartagena, Colombia. Maracaibo, Venezuela.

CANADIAN NATIONAL STEAMSHIPS. Service between Jamaica and Belize, British Honduras.

ELDERS & FYFFES LTD. Calls at Puerto Limon, Costa Rica. Colon, (Cristobal) Panama, as well as at Colombian and Honduras ports.

PART OF
KINGSTON, JAMAICA

Scale 1000 feet = 1 inch

Tram Car Lines - - - - - -

CHAPTER X

ABORIGINES

At the present time there are no native Indians existing on Jamaica, and there are practically no inhabitants showing distinctive characteristics of aboriginal blood. When Columbus first landed on Jamaica he found it thickly inhabited with peaceful, friendly Indians who were still in the stone age. Just what race or tribe they belonged to is not definitely known, but it is generally supposed that they were an offshoot of the Arowaks.

Just how many Indians inhabited Jamaica at the time of its settlement by the Spaniards is impossible to state, but the probability is that there were at least four or five hundred thousand. Unfortunately for them they were not a fighting lot, and mistook the Spaniards for friends. As a result, the Dons not only killed them by wholesale, but made slaves of all those left alive; so that, by the time the British took Jamaica in 1655, only a handful of aborigines were left on the island, and, a few years later, not an Indian remained.

In many portions of Jamaica remains of these extinct aborigines are common. Largely the relics

[171]

consist of polished stone ax-heads or celts; stone images and stone *metates* or grinding-stones similar to those of Mexico and Central America; unglazed pottery of rather plain design; rock carvings, and a few articles of wood found in caves. A few skeletons and skulls have been found, all of which show evidences of artificial malformation of the skulls. According to Spanish accounts, the Jamaican natives were similar to those on the other islands. They dwelt in thatched houses, slept in hammocks, and cultivated maize, cotton, yams, bananas, pineapples and other fruits and vegetables, and also eked out their larder by hunting and fishing. Apparently they did not use bows and arrows.

Of the language of the aborigines little or nothing is known, and in only a few cases are there Indian names in use today. Xmayca, is the best known, as corrupted in the island's name, but it is probable that several other place names also are corruptions of those used by the aborigines.

Agriculture

Jamaica is primarily and principally dependent upon agriculture. Although various minerals occur, and copper, iron, gold, etc., have been mined on the island, the real riches of Jamaica are its fertile soil, its climate and its abundant water supply which enable almost any tropical and semi-tropical and many temperate zone economic plants to be raised to perfection.

SUGAR. In former years sugar was the mainstay of the island and, with its attendant products, molasses and rum, it brought fortunes to the planters. But today sugar and sugar products have dropped to second place and bananas are the leading crop. In fact the bananas form more than one half the total exports of the island at the present time.

BANANAS. Numerous varieties of bananas are raised in Jamaica, but the variety grown for export is the Gros Michel or Martinique, which is the best suited to rough handling and has the advantages of remaining upon the stem even after fully ripe and of ripening well and evenly when picked green. In the more mountainous districts many of the China or Cavendish bananas are grown. This is a shorter, stouter fruit, and, although many persons consider it a far finer banana than the Gros Michel, it does not sell so well in the northern markets. Red bananas which northerners—for some inexplicable reason—consider a great delicacy, and which are always expensive, are grown but little for export. Very largely this is due to the fact that twice as much time is required for the red variety to reach maturity and bear as for the yellow. Moreover, the bunches are smaller, and, as bananas are always purchased from the planters on the basis of the number of "hands" on a bunch, the larger the bunches produced per tree the more profitable the crop. Unfortunately, for those who never visit the lands where bananas are grown, the varieties shipped north are about the coarsest and poorest of all. There are scores of varieties far more delicate, more tender, sweeter and better flavored than the Gros Michel or Cavendish. Especially is this true of the several varieties of the so-called "fig-bananas" or "ladies' fingers." These are very small, with paper-thin skins, deliciously tender and sweet and with flavors like pears or apples.

As these fig-bananas ripen one or two at a time, and drop from the bunch as fast as ripe, it is next to impossible to ship them. Finally there is the fact that the average northerner eats his bananas long before they are really ripe. A banana unless fully ripe is most indigestible, while if fully ripe it is readily digested; but a banana is not in its best condition until it is beginning to turn black, or has black patches or spots on its yellow skin. Until the black spots show, the fruit is still green.

COFFEE is produced in many parts of Jamaica and stands third in the value of the island's exports. Blue Mountain coffee is considered one of the finest and highest priced coffees in the world, but not all of Jamaica's coffee is of this grade by any means.

PIMENTO or ALLSPICE is indigenous to Jamaica

and at one time was the second most important crop of the island. Pimento stands fourth in value of the island's agricultural exports.

COCONUTS are extensively grown and, with the dried meat or COPRA, form the fifth in Jamaica's agricultural products.

COCOA, or more properly CACAO, is the sixth most valuable of Jamaica's crops.

LOGWOOD and DYEWOODS are an important product of Jamaica, although never cultivated, the wild trees being cut and shipped or transformed to extract on the island.

TOBACCO. Although in the United States Jamaican tobacco and cigars are almost unknown, many excellent judges declare them equal to the average Cuban or Puerto Rican product, and in the Canal Zone they have an enormous sale.

SISAL or HENNEQUIN is grown most successfully in the drier portions of Jamaica, and there is a factory for the manufacture of sisal rope, twine, matting, bagging, etc.

MISCELLANEOUS PRODUCTS. Among the other important agricultural products of Jamaica are HONEY, GINGER—which is a minor product although in the minds of many persons more closely associated with Jamaica than any other product—SARSAPARILLA, KOLA NUTS, ANATTO, ARROWROOT, CASHEW NUTS, CASSAVA, TAPIOCA, and various tropical fruits, as well as dried bananas. For home consumption—and for limited export—Jamaica produces MAIZE, GUINEA GRASS, PEAS, BEANS, CABBAGES, POTATOES, SWEET POTATOES, YAMS, OKRA, CARROTS, TURNIPS, TOMATOES, PEPPERS, EGGPLANTS, PUMPKINS, LETTUCE, RADISHES—practically all the vegetables of the tropical and temperate zones. Cattle, sheep, swine, and poultry are raised in large quantities and dairy farming is an important industry.

The following is the value of the various leading agricultural exports of Jamaica for 1928 (an average year):

Bananas	£1,773,695
Sugar (raw)	709,848
Coffee	378,118
Pimento	283,622
Coconuts and copra	233,527
Cocoa	110,011
Logwood extracts	90,494
Logwood	84,745
Ginger (dry)	83,871
Rum	78,831
Grapefruit	53,356
Tobacco and cigars	46,283
Essential oils	43,287

In addition to all these, considerable quantities are exported of the following: HIDES, SKINS, WOOD and TIMBER (ebony, satin wood, fustic, lignum-vitæ), BEESWAX, DIVI-DIVI, LIME JUICE, TORTOISE

SHELL, TURTLE (dried), NUTMEGS and SPICES, PRE-
SERVES, etc.

At one time there were high hopes of making
cinchona (quinine) a very lucrative industry, but
the experiment was not a success commercially.

Today extensive experiments are being made at
rearing silk worms and producing silk.

ARCHITECTURE

As there are very few of the old Spanish buildings remaining in Jamaica, and almost as few of
the buildings erected by the earlier British settlers, the architectural features of the island are,
as a rule, fairly modern and are not particularly
striking or typical. It is very questionable if a
single authentic Spanish building or work remains.
Here and there are so-called Spanish bridges and
wells, but even these have been repaired from
time to time, and little of the original remains. The
principal towns erected by the Spaniards were
Melilla, the first town founded by them, near
Port Maria; Sevilla Nueva, near St. Ann's Bay;
and Spanish Town or Villa de la Vega as the Dons
called it.

Regarding the type of buildings in these Spanish towns, we have the description given by Sir
Hans Sloane who was in Jamaica thirty-three
years after it was acquired by the British. According to him, they were: "Usually one storey

high, having a porch, parlour and each end a room with small ones behind. They built with posts put deep in the ground; on the sides their houses were plastered up with clay or reeds, or made of the split trunks of cabbage trees (palms) nailed close to one another, and were covered with tiles or palmetto thatch. The lowness as well as fixing the posts deep in the earth was for fear their houses should be ruined by earthquakes, as well as for coolness."

Of the ecclesiastical edifices in the Spanish capital—Spanish Town—there are trustworthy records of only an abbey and two chapels—one of the Red and the other of the White Cross. The present cathedral is on the site of the former. Both the chapels were of brick, but the historian, Long, states that he saw in the town, "many large stone mouldings for the bases of columns and other portions of columns as well as sculptures." He also states that the sculptured stonework dug from the ruins of Sevilla Nueva had been executed by expert sculptors. So perhaps the Dons planned to erect more imposing edifices than those that existed at the time of the British conquest. In 1739, Charles Leslie wrote: "The gentlemen's houses are generally built low of one storey consisting of five or six handsome apartments beautifully lined and floored with mahogany. In the towns are several houses of two storeys, but that way of build-

View from the grounds of Hotel Titchfield, overlooking the harbor

The Patio at the Constant Spring Hotel, beautifully situated near the capital city, Kingston

ing is disapproved because they seldom are known to stand the shock of earthquake or the fury of a storm."

Of modern buildings, the church at Spanish Town has no architectural beauty. The so-called King's House at Spanish Town, built in 1762, and almost totally destroyed by fire in 1926, was at one time deemed "the best and noblest edifice of its kind in North America or any of the British colonies in the West Indies." But a better appreciation than this, of Long's, is that given by Monk Lewis in 1834, who said: "It is a large, clumsy-looking building with a portico . . . and it can advance no pretensions to architectural beauty." The façade was two hundred feet long, the free-stone of which it was constructed having come from the Hope River course. The columns of the portico were of Portland stone, the pavement of white marble.

Hakewell, writing in 1821, said: "The handsomest building in Kingston is the Scotch church in Duke Street." Of Montego Bay, he said: "The church of this town is the handsomest on the island." Yet the church is a strange hodge-podge of Classic and Gothic architecture with an excrescence-like portico addition on one side.

One reason why the houses of the period were not noteworthy for their artistic appearance was because they were as much forts as homes and were provided with loopholes, often fortified by guns, and were even at times surrounded by walls and a moat (as at Colbeck Castle).

About the middle of the eighteenth century three or four wealthy Kingston merchants wagered among themselves as to who could build the most magnificent mansion. The results were Harmony Hall (since rebuilt); the present Technical School; Jasper Hall or Constantine House, destroyed by the earthquake of 1907; and Headquarters House, formerly known as Hibbert's House.

Kingston itself was laid out by Col. Christian Lilly in 1695, in the form of a square with streets at right angles. But various lanes were added, and arcades or *portales* were built as a protection from the sun, regardless of the architectural effect. In the minds of most persons the earthquake of 1907 had one good result; it razed the hodgepodge into which Kingston had grown and gave an opportunity to rebuild the city with structures adapted architecturally to a tropical country where earthquakes are liable to occur. But, unfortunately, reinforced concrete was not much in vogue at the time, and, as a result, Kingston, although vastly improved in many ways, is far from being an ideal city for a tropical earthquaky land.

About the only noteworthy buildings erected as a result of the destruction of Kingston were the new King's House, the Government Buildings, the

[180]

Bank of Nova Scotia, the Royal Mail Office Building, the Institute of Jamaica, the Roman Catholic Cathedral and the Parish Church. However, many of the private residences are well designed and artistically colored, while the more recent buildings are largely of reinforced concrete.

BAGGAGE (See Railways)

BASKETS

Hand baskets of many sizes and shapes, locally called "bankra," are obtainable. They are made of various materials, such as palmetto leaves, Jipijapa palm, banana bark, bamboo, wire-grass, etc. Some are quite attractive, especially those colored with anato and other native vegetable dyes.

BATHING (See Sports)

BATHS (See Mineral Springs)

BOOKS AND MAGAZINES

Although Jamaicans cannot be said to be a very literary lot, almost any of the latest works of fiction and many of the British and American periodicals are obtainable. The best library is that of the Institute of Jamaica with its three thousand members. The Institute practically supplies the island with its reading matter, sending out boxes of books to fifty branch institutions and to literary societies and school teachers' associations throughout the island. Largely the books in use are British, especially the various volumes of the "Colonial Library" and other editions. Many of the schools have quite large libraries of their own.

Cayman Islands

A group of three small islands: Grand Cayman, Little Cayman and Cayman Brac, situated about one hundred and eighty miles northwest of Jamaica and a dependency of the latter.

Grand Cayman, the largest of the three, is about seventeen miles long by four to eight miles wide. The others are each about ten miles long and a mile wide and are about seven miles apart and seventy miles from Grand Cayman. All are low—nowhere more than fifty feet above sea level—but well wooded, with fairly fertile soil, and are rather attractive.

Discovered by Columbus, May 10, 1503, they were named "Las Tortugas" on account of the great numbers of sea-turtles found on the islands by the Spaniards.

Very early in the history of the Caribbean, the Caymans became a favorite resort of the buccaneers and, in later years, of pirates. They were colonized mainly by men from Jamaica, some of them buccaneers and others royalists fleeing from the Cromwellian rule; and the present-day inhabitants are mainly descendants of these men and their slaves. Unlike most of the West Indies, the white inhabitants have maintained their purity of blood to a great extent, and the percentage of whites in the population is greater than in any other British West Indian colony. The total population of the islands is about six thousand, of whom fully five thousand live on Grand Cayman.

Although so similar in all respects, and so near together, there is little intercourse or sympathy between the three islands. In many respects the Caymans are very backward and untouched by modernities, yet there are good roads on Grand Cayman and there are over seventy automobiles on the island. There are also electric light plants, ice factories, radios, etc. The principal exports are coconuts, turtles, mahogany, cedar, dyewoods, etc. The turtles are mainly from the Central American coast and are brought alive to the Caymans where they are confined in pens or "crawls" (a corruption of the Spanish "corral") until sold.

Georgetown, on Grand Cayman, is the capital of the group. Other important settlements are West Bay and Boddentown.

Until comparatively recently the Caymans were rather inaccessible and could be reached only by occasional sail boats from Jamaica or Central America; but there is now a regular weekly service of excellent motor boats between Jamaica and the Caymans, while there is irregular communication with the Isle of Pines.

[183]

The language is English, spoken with a peculiar accent by the natives. Currency as in Jamaica.

CLIMATE

The temperature is very equable. There are no sudden rises and falls, such as occur in Cuba and Florida. Nights are cooler than days, but there is very little variation in actual temperature, the apparent coolness being due largely to the absence of the sun and the night breeze. Even in summer and winter the thermometer varies very slightly. Although this is true of practically all portions of the island, it is particularly noticeable at elevations of between two and five thousand feet, where the extreme range of temperature is rarely greater than twelve or thirteen degrees Fahrenheit.

There are very few days when the sun does not shine. Even in the rather short rainy seasons (May and October) hardly a day passes without some sunshine. As a result, even after a heavy rain the streets and roads dry very quickly and the people give little heed to rainy weather. Despite the ardent and almost continual sunshine, sunstrokes or heat prostrations are almost unknown. Even in the lowlands, where the highest temperatures prevail, the heat is almost always relieved by the trade wind, or "Doctor" as it is appropriately called by the natives.

In respect to rainfall Jamaica has several distinct rain zones. In a general way the southern portions of the island are dry, the vicinity of Kingston having an annual rainfall of from thirty to thirty-five inches, while other portions of the island record from forty inches to as high as one hundred inches or more per annum.

Owing to the equable temperature, the entire absence of cold air, and the fact that Jamaica is in the Caribbean Sea, the sea water is uniformly about eighty degrees both day and night, winter and summer.

Average yearly temperature at sea level, 78°–79° F.; at 3000 feet, 68°–69° F.; at 7388 feet, 55° F. (the highest point on the island).

Heaviest annual rainfall recorded: Portland, northeastern portion of island—200 inches.

The highest temperature ever recorded in Kingston was 97.8° F., on August 11, 1923.

The heaviest rainfall ever recorded in Kingston was 8.93 inches in twenty-four hours, 30.45 inches in one month and 68.11 inches in the entire year (1909).

CLOTHING

Visitors to Jamaica should provide themselves with light summer clothing—ducks, drills or Palm Beach suits for men, and muslins, light silks and organdies for women; but medium-weight clothes and light wraps should be carried also, for in the mountains, the nights—especially if driving or motoring—are cool. Of course those who plan to indulge in outdoor sports should carry suitable outfits. Dress suits and evening gowns should be provided.

Cost of Wintering in Jamaica

The cost of spending the winter in Jamaica (say three months) can be estimated, according to individual requirements, on the following basis:—

	From England.			From New York.	
Return Fare (1st Class)	£60,	£50,	£34 *	$204.00 or	$160.00
Accommodation at £7 ($35.00), per week, for 12 weeks	£84,	£84,	£84	$420.00	$420.00
	£144,	£134,	£118	$624.00	$580.00

The above cost will be exceeded if accommodation is taken at the largest hotels and lessened if one stays in a boarding-house or private home.

Rates for accommodation in hotels and boarding-houses, etc., vary from about £2 ($10.00) per week to as much per day.

To the above figures would have to be added the cost of traveling in Jamaica (see paragraph on Cost of Tours, above), personal requirements, etc.

A stay can be made of any duration in any particular part of the island, and expenses reduced to

* (The boats of the Jamaica Direct Fruit Line Ltd., offer an intermediate class costing £34 return.)

a minimum so that it should be as cheap to live in Jamaica as in England, Canada or the U.S.A.

COUNTIES AND THEIR CHIEF POINTS OF INTEREST

Visitors to Jamaica hear a great deal about the various parishes, but very seldom do they hear the counties mentioned, although the latter are more important when arranging tours or trips to various places.

The island is divided into fourteen parishes and three counties—Cornwall, Middlesex and Surrey —each of which has its distinctive features. In a way the counties are analogous to our states, while the parishes may be compared to our counties.

Of the three counties in Jamaica, Surrey has an area of 827 square miles and contains the parishes of Portland, St. Thomas and Port Royal, as well as Kingston. It is the only county containing mountains over 4000 feet in height and is the most scenic of the three, including as it does the eastern end of the island with the Blue Mountains.

The chief localities and places of interest in Surrey are:

Kingston, the capital.
Hope Botanic Gardens.
King's House, residence of the governor.
Cane River Falls near Kingston.

[187]

Port Royal.

Stony Hill and the Rio Pedro to Glengoffe, etc.

Gordon Town, Guava Ridge, Mavis Bank and the Blue Mountains Peak.

Flamstead and Bellevue.

Newcastle, Hardwar Gap, 4079 feet. Buff Bay River.

Catherine's Peak, 5060 ft.

Silver Hill, Chalybeate Spring (formerly a spa) Pleasant Hill.

Cinchona Hill Gardens. Botanic Gardens, 5017 feet.

Rozelle, Morant Bay, Port Morant, Bath (mineral springs).

Cuna Cuna Pass and John Crow Mountains.

Manchioneal (where Michael Scott wrote "Tom Cringle's Log").

Port Antonio.

Blue Hole.

Rio Grande River Valley.

Rafting on Rio Grande.

Moore Town (home of the Maroons).

Middlesex County has an area of 2060 square miles and contains the parishes of St. Mary, St. Catherine, Clarendon, Manchester and St. Ann. It is famed for its oranges, and is largely rolling upland country. It contains many places of historic interest and great beauty, among them being:

[188]

Spanish Town with its old Government Buildings, English Cathedral (oldest in British West Indies), Memorials, etc.

Bog Walk.

Riverside and Natural Bridge.

Moneague, 1000 feet.

Claremont.

St. Ann's Bay.

Brown's Town.

Columbus Cove, Ocho Rios, Runaway Bay and Dry Harbour, all associated with Spanish colonial days.

Dunn's River Falls and bathing beach and Roaring River Falls.

Fern Gully.

Castleton Botanic Gardens.

Port Maria.

Alligator Pond, Spur Tree Hill, Caves, etc.

Christiana, highest part of Middlesex.

Milk River mineral baths where treatment may be obtained.

Mandeville, noted for its climate and scenery.

The County of Cornwall has an area of 1563 square miles and contains the parishes of St. Elizabeth, Trelawny, St. James, Hanover and Westmoreland. Montego Bay is in this parish, as are the following places of interest:

Rose Hall.

Lucea, with the drive from Montego Bay to Green Island.

The Martha Brae near Falmouth, a fishing resort.

Beauty spots on road from Montego Bay to Brown's Town.

The Cockpit Country, once the haunt of brigands and Maroons.

Accompong, the Maroon capital.

Maggotty Waterfall.

Bamboo Avenue at Lacovia.

Black River, a paradise for anglers.

Malvern, 2200 feet.

Shettlewood, a cattle ranch.

Dolphin Head, 1816 feet, the highest point in western Jamaica.

CHIEF CITIES AND TOURIST CENTERS

KINGSTON. Population about 65,000. Capital of Jamaica. On the south coast with the finest harbor in the West Indies.

PORT ANTONIO. Population about 6500. Second only to Kingston as a port. Distance from Kingston by railway 75 miles; by road 62 miles. On north coast. Greatest shipping point for bananas.

MONTEGO BAY. An important seaport. Population about 7000. Distance from Kingston by railway 113 miles; by road 130 miles. On northwest coast.

MONEAGUE. Population about 3000. About 1000 feet above the sea. By rail to Edwarton Station 29 miles from Kingston, thence by road 8 miles.

MANDEVILLE. Population about 2000. About 2000 feet above the sea. By rail to Williamsfield and thence by road 61 miles from Kingston.

CURRENCY

Although British money—pounds, shillings and pence—is the legal and official currency of Jamaica, yet everyone is familiar with dollars and cents. Most accounts are kept in the British monetary system and British coins of all denominations—gold, silver and copper—are in general use and are, officially, the legal tender of the island; but American gold, silver and paper money is always current and acceptable, the dollar being reckoned at four shillings. American coins of less than twenty-five cents are not generally accepted.

In addition to the British and United States coins, there are local Jamaican nickels of one penny, one half penny and one farthing.

The paper money in circulation consists of Barclay's Bank, Royal Bank of Canada, Bank of Nova Scotia and Canadian Bank of Commerce notes, as well as British Treasury notes of one pound and ten shillings value, and local (Jamaican) currency notes of ten shillings and five shillings.

Persons unaccustomed to using British coins should be careful not to confuse the Jamaican nickel penny with the British florin (two-shilling piece) or the Jamaican half penny with the British shilling. They are readily distinguished even in the dark, as the Jamaican coins are not milled but have smooth edges, whereas the British coins have milled edges.

British weights and measures are used—most weights of over one hundred pounds being figured in "stones" or "hundredweights."

Customs and Duties

Temporary visitors to Jamaica are allowed to bring in, free of duties and restrictions, anything they may require for their personal use, other than automobiles, firearms, and fishing tackle. In the case of such articles, free entry is permitted for a period of three months, upon a deposit being made equal to thirty per cent of the assessed duty. This deposit is returned when the goods are taken out of the country, within the stipulated three months. After that period five per cent of the duty is deducted from the deposit for each month beyond the three months, and at the expiration of six months full duty is collected.

Jamaica's customs tariff admits free of duty the following: Magazines, newspapers, books, artificial limbs, coal and packages for island products;

agricultural tools and implements and machinery, sewing machines, artisans' tools for preparing local products for exportation to countries of preferential tariff. Otherwise there is a duty of five per cent.

Specifically rated imports on which fixed duties are charged, include wines, spirits, butter, cheese, meat, fish not in tins, oils, gasoline, ale, tea, tobacco, sugar, etc.

All other goods are assessed at ad valorem duties of from ten to twenty per cent.

Although spirits, tobacco, cigars and cigarettes are dutiable, the Jamaican customs officers are most courteous and liberal and visitors are permitted to bring in a reasonable amount for their personal use.

Doctors

Prospective visitors to Jamaica need have no fear of being ill and unable to secure adequate medical attention. There are excellent physicians and surgeons in all the important centers on the island.

Education

Northern visitors to Jamaica (as to the other British West Indies) invariably comment on the excellent English spoken by the natives. Unless of the most illiterate peasant class, even the blacks use English grammatically, even if with a strong negro accent. But, considering the educational advantages and the natives' almost universal desire to become educated, this is not surprising. The Jamaica elementary schools number six hundred and seventy-five, divided as follows:

Government,	124
Church of England,	174
Baptist,	107
Wesleyan,	71
Moravian,	57
Church of Scotland,	6
Presbyterian,	51
Congregational,	19
Methodist,	7
American Missionary,	5
Roman Catholic,	30
Society of Friends,	5
Undenominational,	15
No denomination,	1

There are also ten endowed secondary schools and a few others with government grants. Athletics, sports, games and physical culture, as well as hygiene, manual training, cookery, etc., are all featured. Government industrial schools provide for the care and education of orphaned and homeless children.

Kingston looking toward the harbor

Newcastle, Jamaica

There are teachers' training colleges, a farm school which furnishes an excellent agricultural training, and a governmental technical and commercial school, besides a number of private commercial schools.

Among the scholarships is a Rhodes Scholarship of £400 ($2000) per annum. The best comment upon Jamaica's educational system is the fact that many natives, graduated on the island, have attained to the highest possible positions in their respective spheres, both in Jamaica and in Europe, Canada and the United States, where they hold responsible positions in business or are successful professional men.

Latest available records show that, with a total population of 900,000, there is an average attendance of over 75,000 children out of a total of the 123,000 of school age. The total annual expenditure on education amounts to nearly £170,000 ($850,000) or practically $1.00 per capita of the entire population. The system of schools and education is based upon the English code, and particular stress is laid upon nature studies and school garden work. All children are entitled to eight years' free education, but efforts at compulsory attendance have proved impractical.

Most of the teachers are natives of Jamaica who have been trained in the four island training colleges. The Shortwood College is maintained at government expense for thirty-six women students.

The Moravian College at Bethlehem can train twenty-five women, while the Roman Catholic College of St. Joseph can accommodate six women.

A Child Welfare Association at Kingston maintains a day nursery, children's home and kindergarten.

The system of education, beyond the elementary schools, is that any child showing exceptional ability or ambition may secure free education in the secondary schools and may acquire a university career as provided by the Jamaica scholarship.

FISHING (See Sports)

FOOTBALL (See Sports)

GEOGRAPHY (See Physical Characters)

GEOLOGY (See Physical Characters)

GOLF (See Sports)

GOVERNMENT

The present political constitution of Jamaica consists of a Governor, a Privy Council and a Legislative Council.

The Governor is appointed by the Sovereign and the tenure of office is usually about six years.

The Privy Council consists of the Senior Military Officer, the Colonial Secretary, the Attorney General and other persons not to exceed eight in number, named by the Sovereign or provisionally appointed by the Governor, subject to approval by the Sovereign. The tenure of office is limited to five years.

The Legislative Council consists of the Governor as President; five *ex-officio* members, the Senior Military Officer, the Colonial Secretary, the Attorney General, the Director of Public Works and the Collector General; nominated members not exceeding ten, and fourteen elected members —one for each Parish. The qualifications of elected members are that they shall have resided in an electoral district for one year or possess an annual income of one hundred and fifty pounds (seven hundred and fifty dollars) or more derived from the land of the parish.

Voters must be British subjects, twenty-one years of age or more, suffering no legal incapacity, and who occupy, as owners or tenants, house property upon which taxes of at least ten shillings are paid or who have a salary of at least fifty pounds (two hundred dollars) a year, or an income of the same amount yearly, arising from business. Women, twenty-five years of age or more, with certain qualifications, are also eligible as voters.

HEALTH.

As a whole, Jamaica is a most healthful island and is, in fact, a real health resort. But among the colored people and blacks there is a great deal of sickness, and the mortality is far too high. Owing to the work of the International Health Board, hookworm and other affections prevalent among the lower classes have been greatly reduced. For the visitor, Jamaica can truthfully be recommended as fully as healthful as our own country. In fact, climatically, it is more healthful, while infectious diseases of any sort are rare, and even malaria is not at all prevalent. Excellent physicians and surgeons, as well as public and private hospitals and nursing homes, are in Kingston, and there are government hospitals in all the principal towns.

HORSE RACES (See Sports)

HOTELS AND BOARDING-HOUSES

There are innumerable hotels, pensions and boarding-houses in every city and town of any importance in Jamaica. Indeed, Jamaica possesses the best hotel accommodations in the British West Indies. Regardless of one's financial status, a hotel can always be found to suit one's purse; for prices range from eight to ten dollars a day, at such establishments as the Titchfield at Port Antonio and the Myrtle Bank at Kingston, to as low as eight or ten dollars a week at some of the smaller, less pretentious, but fully as comfortable places in the mountain towns.

JAMAICA OF TODAY

Hunting (See Sports)

Immigration Laws

No immigration laws affect English-speaking visitors or prospective settlers in Jamaica. American citizens do not require visas on passports, if merely transitory visitors. The immigration laws prohibit the entry of undesirables, persons suffering from certain diseases and certain races. Otherwise all are welcome.

Imports and Exports

For the year 1927 (last available figures) Jamaica's imports amounted to a value of	£6,001,768	($30,008,840)
Total exports for the year	£4,857,750	($24,288,750)
Total	£10,859,518	($54,297,590)

The distribution of exports was as follows:

To United Kingdom	18.9%
" United States	41.7%
" Canada	17.5%
" Other countries	21.9%

Of the total exports BANANAS accounted for	48.9%
" " " " Sugar " "	16.4%
" " " " Coffee " "	6.6%

The remaining amount, approximately 28%, was made up of a great variety of products, including allspice, coconuts, copra, dyewoods, logwood extract, dyes, cocoa, timber, rum, spices, nutmegs, grapefruit, oranges, limes, lime juice, essential

[199]

oils, hides and skins, lard, annotto, honey, wax, turtle shell, dried meats, preserves, etc.

Over two thousand vessels, with a total tonnage of more than three million tons, enter and leave the Jamaican ports annually.

INSECTS

Although insects are exceedingly abundant in Jamaica, as in all tropical countries, the noxious or troublesome insect pests are by no means as bad as in many of the West Indies. Ants, of course, are everywhere, and over forty species are known on the island; but only three or four are peculiar to Jamaica, the others being species found nearly everywhere. Although ants may be a great nuisance, yet they are very useful and do far more good than harm. Thus the large, savage-looking fellows, so common under stones, flower pots, etc., in Jamaica, prey upon the destructive white ants or termites, which are perhaps the greatest of tropical pests. The common fire-ant or stinging-ant of Jamaica devours the eggs and larvæ of the house fly. Another species devours the scale insects on citrus trees.

Perhaps the most striking of Jamaican ants are the so-called parasol or leaf-cutting ants, three kinds being found in Jamaica. These may be seen hurrying along in files, each ant with a bit of leaf or flower held like a sunshade over its head. On reaching the nest the ants chew the leaves into a pulp, which is suspended from the roof of the underground chamber. Then the ants plant the spores of a fungus in the mass, which serves them for a mushroom bed. The mushrooms thus grown by the ants, and upon which they feed, are tiny pearl-like bodies.

There are six species of house ants in Jamaica, but with care food may be kept out of their reach. In Jamaica it is customary to suspend food-safes from the ceiling by means of fine wires wrapped with cloths saturated with oil, or to place the legs of food-safes in tins filled with kerosene. Tight, all-metal refrigerators also keep out the ants, and the liberal use of "Flit" or some similar compound will be found a great help.

MOSQUITOES are numerous in some localities, especially along the sea-shore, and after rains these pests are often troublesome. As far as known all the Jamaican anopheles mosquitoes—those carrying malaria—are confined to the lowlands, and no specimens of the four known species have been taken at an altitude of over one thousand feet. The yellow fever mosquito is not known to exist in Jamaica.

COCKROACHES. There are fully a dozen kinds of these insects in Jamaica, but only three or four are house pests. The largest species, known as "drummers," often enter houses at night in large swarms, especially after a rain, but they are not strictly household cockroaches, and most of them soon leave the buildings. Those that remain, however, do a great deal of damage to clothing, draperies, etc.

CRICKETS also enter the houses and eat holes in textiles, especially if the cloth has spots of dirt or grease upon it.

FLIES. Many species of troublesome flies occur in Jamaica, but they are not so bad as in our northern states during the summer. The common house fly, the meat flies, blue-bottles, etc., are common. In addition there are biting flies, black flies, and midges or gnats which are very troublesome at certain times in some localities.

TICKS. Ticks are pests where there are cattle or domestic animals, but the wood-ticks that will attack human beings are not so numerous as in most tropical countries.

BUTTERFLIES. Although most persons imagine the tropics as teeming with gorgeous butterflies and moths, the butterflies of the American tropics are neither so numerous nor so gorgeous as is generally supposed. There are less than one hundred species of butterflies found on Jamaica, and comparatively few of these are brilliantly or strikingly colored. In fact the butterflies as a whole are not so brilliant or handsome as our own. The majority are rather small, yellow, brown, white or blue species. But there are several large papilios, or swallowtails, and in the mountains there are several magnificent species, the rarest and finest being the *Papilio homerus*. A very fine collection of moths and butterflies is in the museum of the Jamaica Institute.

SCORPIONS are common, but are neither troublesome nor dangerous. Largely they are small species living among dead wood, under stones and logs, etc. There are also still smaller pale-colored house scorpions that should be protected rather than destroyed, as they devour great numbers of ants, termites, cockroaches, bedbugs and other vermin. The sting of the scorpion has been vastly exaggerated, and even the sting inflicted by the largest specimens is no worse than the sting of a good lively hornet.

CENTIPEDES. The large venomous centipedes are rather rare in Jamaica. Many persons have resided in the island for years and never have seen one. They are never numerous enough to prove troublesome, and their so-called "sting" (in reality a bite) is neither very painful nor very poisonous; not half as bad as the sting of a bumble-bee.

LAND SHELLS.

Next to Cuba, Jamaica is the richest island in the world in land shells. About five hundred species are known from the island and nearly all are peculiar to Jamaica. The Vendryes Collection of Jamaican land shells, which is credited with being the finest in the world, is in the Institute of Jamaica museum.

MAGAZINES (See Books)

MANUFACTURES

Although there are no large manufacturing plants in Jamaica, there are many small factories and works engaged in manufacturing various articles from the island's produce. Among these are: a cigar factory in Kingston, a tile factory, a sisal hemp factory; dye works, starch factories, iron foundries, printing works; biscuit factories, bottling works, furniture factories, potteries, tanneries, as well as hat-making industries, basket making, creameries, ice-making plants, gas works, machine shops, saw mills, brick yards, soap factories, and plants for the preparation of spices, dried and preserved fruits, essential oils, guava jelly, etc.

MILITARY.

At the present time the troops in Jamaica consist of a company of Royal Artillery and Royal Engineers and a battalion of a British infantry regiment, with the accompanying medical, ordnance, and army service corps. The local forces consist of the Jamaica Militia Artillery, an Engineer Corps, Kingston Infantry Volunteers, the

Jamaica Military (formerly West Indian Regiment) Band, the Jamaica Reserve Regiment, and a reserve corps of scouts.

The Royal Navy Dockyard at Port Royal, which had been famous for two hundred and fifty years, was officially closed in 1905. No naval vessels are permanently stationed at Jamaica, but the ships of the British North American and West Indies Squadrons make annual visits, and other British men-of-war make frequent calls. United States war vessels frequently visit Jamaica.

MINERAL SPRINGS AND BATHS

For over a century the baths of St. Thomas the Apostle and those at Milk River have borne an enviable reputation. In 1916, the late Dr. Earle, health officer at Port Royal, declared that the Milk River baths are among the most remarkable in the world. Extraordinary cures have been accredited to both the above baths. An analysis of the waters of the Milk River baths show its radio activity is comparatively as follows:

```
 9 times as active as Bath, England.
50   "     "     "    " Vichy, France.
 3   "     "     "    " Karlsbad, Austria.
54   "     "     "    " Baden, Switzerland.
```

The Milk River baths originate in warm, saline springs with a temperature of 92° F. Analyses of the waters show the contents to be as follows:

	Parts per 100,000
Calcium	60.03
Magnesium	69.49
Sodium	784.77
Sulphate	189.30
Bicarbonate	10.06
Silica	1.20
Chloride	1,375.00
	2,489.85

The residue is composed of potassium, lithium, bromine, etc. Radio activity is equal to 160.2 × 10–10 curies per liter or 43.25 Maché units.

The spring at Bath, in St. Thomas parish, is the hottest on the island, the water having a temperature of 126° to 128° F. at the spring, although considerably cooler at the baths. This is a sulphuric spring and contains a great deal of hydro-sulphate of lime. The waters are not purgative and are considered very beneficial for gout, rheumatism, gravel, cutaneous diseases and fevers. The analysis shows the following contents:

[206]

	Parts per 100,000, hot bath.	Per 100,000, cold bath.
Calcium	2.60	5.02
Magnesium	0.15	0.98
Sodium	14.80	10.45
Sulphate	11.10	3.41
Bicarbonate	1.68	10.98
Carbonate	0.60	——
Silica	3.70	4.90
Chloride	18.00	19.00

Radio activity in curies per liter 4.9 X, 10-10; 0.09X, 10–10.

The flow of the Milk River baths is over 300,000 gallons a day. The Spa Spring or Jamaica Spa at Silver Hill, in the parish of St. Andrew, was at one time maintained as a government institution, with extensive buildings. The waters of this spring are aerated, cold, chalybeate, tonic and are beneficial in cases of debility, in dropsy and in stomach troubles.

At Rockfort, in the parish of Kingston, there is a mineral spring at the edge of the sea; but little is known as to its medicinal properties. There is also a spring on the Adams River near Downer's Hut Gap, and at Moffat there is a spring on the White River. In Portland, on the Guava River there is another spring, while at Windsor in St. Ann there is a spring that at one time was very popular. In Hanover there is a hot spring at Buxton on the Cabaritta River, and there are still others at Lower Works in St. Elizabeth, at St. Faith's in St. Catherine parish, on the Good Hope Estate in St. John's district, and at Port Henderson, the last formerly having been a favorite spa for the residents of Spanish Town.

MONEY (See Currency)

MOTOR CARS IN JAMAICA

There are at present approximately 6000 private motor cars in use in Jamaica, in addition to about 250 taxis, 1500 motor trucks and 550 motor cycles, making a total of about 8300 motor-driven vehicles in addition to those brought in and used by temporary visitors to the island.

MUSIC

Aside from church and society musical entertainments, an occasional light opera or musical comedy by local talent, and touring opera companies from England or Italy, there is little in the way of musical attractions in Jamaica; but the band of the West Indian Regiment is world famed, and when the regiment itself was disbanded the band was retained and gives frequent concerts.

NAVY (See Military)

PAINTING

There are no very noteworthy paintings in Jamaica, and none of the real masters. A number of interesting drawings by a man named Robins; some very early engravings of Jamaica scenery by an unknown artist, which are dated 1766–70; six water colors by Louis Belanger; some paintings by Philip Wickstead; an aquatint by Merigot from a painting by J. Bourgoin, representing an episode of the Maroon rebellion; a portrait of Sir Chas. Metcalf by Bradish; several paintings by Lady Barkly; a painting of Blue Mountains Peak and one of Liguanea Plain by Kirkpatrick, and "Rodney in Action Aboard the *Formidable*," by R. E. Pine, comprise about all the noteworthy works of art in Jamaica.

PHYSICAL CHARACTERISTICS OF JAMAICA

Jamaica is 144 miles in length with an extreme width of 49 miles and an area of 4450 square miles. Approximately one half of the total area is at an elevation of 1000 feet or more above the sea, while a great deal of the territory is from 2000 to 3000 feet and more above sea level. There are several large plains or savannas, many rich valleys and a number of high table lands or plateaus. But on the whole it is a mountainous island with comparatively little level land except near the coasts. As indicated by its aboriginal name—Xmayca, pronounced Shaymayca—which means a land of springs and waters, Jamaica is well supplied with rivers and streams, none of which, however, are navigable, except for rowboats, canoes or rafts, and only for short distances by such small craft. There are numerous mineral springs on the island, but no true lakes. Although frequently shaken by earthquakes, few of which have been severe, Jamaica cannot be considered volcanic, though there is one spot which it has been claimed is the crater of a very ancient extinct volcano. Broadly speaking the island consists of ancient igneous rocks overlaid with limestone and sedimentary rocks.

Various ores are known to occur, but no mines have been profitably worked since the early Spanish days, if indeed, they were then. That the Spaniards secured a certain amount of silver and gold from Jamaica is proved by documents showing that in 1539, it was decreed by Spain that the silver and gold extracted in Jamaica should be stamped with the royal arms and the word "Jamaica." Moreover, the names Rio de Oro and Rio Cobre would indicate that both metals—gold and copper—were fairly abundant. In all probability the gold obtained was from small placers which were soon worked out. Whether the silver was obtained in smelting copper or from a silver ore is not recorded, as far as known.

Jamaica possesses no very lofty mountains, compared with those of North or South America,

Africa or Asia, the highest point being Blue Mountain Peak, 7360 feet above sea level. But the island's mountains are the third highest in the West Indies, being exceeded only by the Pico de Turquino of Cuba (7600 feet) and by the Loma Tina range of Santo Domingo which towers for over 10,000 feet above the sea. The principal mountains in Jamaica, with their altitudes, are as follows:

	Feet
John Crow Mountains (average height) ..	2100
Cuna Cuna Pass	2698
Blue Mountains Western Peak	7360
Portland Gap	5495
Sir John's Peak	6100
House, Cinchona Plantation	5017
Arntully Gap	2800
Hagley Gap	1959
Morce's Gap	4945
Content Gap	3250
Newcastle Hospital	3800
Flamstead	3660
Belle Vue	3780
Silver Hill Gap	3513
Catherine's Peak	5060
Cold Spring Gap	4500
Hardwar Gap	4380
Fox's Gap	3907
Stony Hill (where road crosses)	1360
Guy's Hill	2100

	Feet
Mt. Diablo (highest point)	2300
” ” (at road crossing)	1800
Bull Head	3000
Mandeville	2060
Accompong	1409
Dolphin Head	1816

Included in the government of Jamaica are the Cayman Islands, Pedro and Morant Cays and Turks and Caicos Islands. The Cayman Islands, about one hundred miles northwest of Jamaica, are low—barely fifty feet above sea level—and consist of Grand Cayman, Little Cayman and Cayman Brac. The Pedro and Morant Cays are uninhabited and are of importance only for their guano. They are about thirty-three miles southeast of Jamaica. The Turks and Caicos Islands are at the extreme southeastern end of the Bahama archipelago and their sole industry is salt.

Kingston's harbor, acknowledged the finest in the British West Indies, has an area of sixteen square miles of which seven square miles have a depth of from seven to ten fathoms. The rise and fall of the tide about Jamaica's coast does not exceed sixteen inches.

Compared with the neighboring islands, Jamaica is about one tenth the size of Cuba and one seventh the size of Santo Domingo.

With its dependencies, it comprises more than one third of the total area of the British West

Indies, with nearly one half of the total population.

PHOTOGRAPHY

Films, cameras and photographic supplies are on sale throughout Jamaica, and numerous firms develop and print films for amateurs. In taking snapshots of Jamaica—or elsewhere in the tropics —care should be used not to under expose. Not only is the light very deceptive, appearing much stronger than it is in reality, but its actinic value is, if anything, less than in the north in summer time. Moreover, there is a great deal of contrast and to avoid solid blacks and whites over-exposure is necessary. The best time to take photographs for good effects is quite early in the morning and late in the afternoon, when the sun's rays are at an angle and not from directly overhead. Do NOT replace exposed films in the tin containers, or moldy, spotted negatives will result.

PLACES OF INTEREST AND AMUSEMENT IN KINGSTON

BANKS

Barclay's Bank, Harbour Street.
Bank of Nova Scotia, King Street.
Royal Bank of Canada, King Street.
Canadian Bank of Commerce, Harbour Street.

CINEMAS
> *The Palace,* Corner of East Queen Street, and South Camp Road.
>
> *The Gaiety.* Corner of East Queen Street and Hanover Street.
>
> *The Movies.* At Cross Roads near Kingston.

BATHING
> At Myrtle Bank Hotel, Bournemouth Bath, etc.

CABLE OFFICE
> The Direct West India Cable Co. Ltd., Royal Mailing Building, Port Royal Street.

CLUBS
> The Jamaica Club, Hanover Street. Residential, Lawn Tennis and Billiards.
>
> Royal Jamaica Yacht Club, Rae Town, Kingston.
>
> St. Andrew Club, Cross Roads, near Kingston. Lawn Tennis, Croquet, Billiards.
>
> The Liguanea Club, Knutsford Park, Halfway Tree Road. Residential, Golf, Tennis, Croquet, Billiards, Swimming.
>
> (Temporary membership may be secured through introduction.)

FISHING
> In harbor.

GOLF
> Liguanea Golf Club and Constant Spring Golf Club.
>
> *Institute of Jamaica.* Museum and Library, Art Gallery, etc. East Street (lower end).

[214]

Jamaica Chamber of Commerce and Merchant's Exchange. Bank of Nova Scotia Building.

NEWSPAPERS

Daily: *The Gleaner.*

Tri-Weekly: *The Jamaica Mail.*
The Northern Weekly News (Montego Bay).

Weekly: *The Jamaica Gazette.*
The Jamaica Times.

Also several monthly magazines.

PARISH CHURCH

Containing grave of Admiral Benbow. Corner of King Street and South Parade. Opposite Victoria Gardens.

POLO

At Up-Park Camp (Military Station), at Knutsford Park and elsewhere.

POST OFFICE

General Post Office Building. Corner of King and Barry Streets, and several branch post offices.

POSTAGE RATES

To U. S. A. and other foreign countries. 2½d. (5c) for first ounce and 1½d (3c.) for each additional ounce.

To England, Canada and British possessions. 1½d. (3c.) for first ounce and 1d (2c.) for each additional ounce.

Inland Letters. 1d. (2c.) per ounce.

[215]

Inland Postcards. ½d. (1c.)

Postcards to all foreign countries and British possessions 1d. (2c.)

Newspapers to all countries. ½d. (1c.) for every two ounces.

Parcel Post between Jamaica and most countries.

RAILWAY STATION

Barry Street, West End.

RACING

At Knutsford Park and at Kingston Race Course.

RESTAURANTS

The chief restaurants are:

Gardner's and The Oleanders, Harbour Street.

Myrtle Bank Hotel, Harbour Street.

The Cabin. Harbour Street.

Barham's Restaurant, Coronation Building.

ROMAN CATHOLIC CATHEDRAL

North Street.

ROWING

Rowboats are for hire at Kingston Harbour. The legal charge is 1 s. (25c.) per person for a trip to a vessel anywhere in the harbor. By the hour, 4 s. ($1)

SHOPPING

Curio and souvenir shops in King Street and Harbour Street.

[216]

TELEPHONE
(Local) at Tourist Bureau, 87 Barry Street.

TELEGRAPH
General Post Office, Corner King and Barry Streets.

TOURIST INFORMATION BUREAU
87 Barry Street.

VICTORIA GARDENS and SOLLAS
(Or Jubilee) Market, King and Orange Streets.

VICTORIA MARKET
Foot of King Street, near harbor.
(Early morning is the best time to visit the markets.)

WARD THEATRE
(Plays, concerts, etc.) North Parade.

POLICE

Jamaica is adequately and most efficiently policed. There are 160 constabulary stations on the island with a force of 1049 officers and constables supplemented by 1093 district constables. There are also special constables, or as we would call them, special police, and detectives. The constables are without exception blacks or colored and are highly efficient, honest, courteous and possess unlimited patience. They are trained and are under the supervision and control of Inspectors of Police who are mainly from Ireland, a land famed for supplying the world with efficient police.

[217]

JAMAICA OF TODAY

POLO (See Sports)

POPULATION

According to the census of 1921 there were 858,118 persons in Jamaica, divided as shown below. Compared with the census of 1911 the figures are interesting as showing the rapid decrease in the white and colored people and the increase of blacks, East Indians and Chinese.

	1911	1921
White	15,605	14,467
Colored	163,201	157,166
Black	630,181	660,250
East Indian	17,380	18,846
Chinese	2,111	3,699
Not stated	2,905	3,690
Total	831,383	858,118

Thus, in a population that was increased by only 26,735 in ten years, the blacks increased by 30,069, or by more individuals than the total increase, while the whites have decreased by 1188 and the colored have decreased by 6035. But the decrease of the whites and colored and the increase of blacks is still more striking by comparing the 1921 figures with those of the census of 1891 which gave the white population as 14,692, the colored as 12,955 and the blacks as only 488,624. In other words, while the white inhabitants have about held their own during the past thirty years, and even slightly increased between 1891 and 1911, the colored people have increased to the extent of 35,211 or over twenty-five per cent, while the blacks have increased by 171,626 or more than thirty-five per cent, which bears out the statement made in Chapter VIII that intermarriage of whites with colored or blacks will inevitably result in the absorption of the white race and the dominance of the black.

But even more alarming, if anything, is the tremendous increase in the numbers of Chinese, an increase of 3218 or nearly seven hundred per cent in thirty years, and an increase by over 2500 in ten years. Judging by these figures, a few more decades will see Jamaica largely Mongolian. According to the 1921 census, there were 203 persons to the square mile; which would make Jamaica more densely populated than Spain, Turkey, Russia or some other European countries, and far more thickly inhabited than Cuba, with but 49 persons to the square mile, or Santo Domingo with only 31.

In addition to the resident population nearly 20,000 tourists visit Jamaica each year.

PORTERS (See Railways)

POTTERY

Visitors looking for artistic pottery as souvenirs of Jamaica will be disappointed. Aside from rather

[219]

crudely made plain or slightly decorated earthen-
ware jars, "monkeys" or water coolers, garden
pots, and bowls or "yabbahs," there is no native
made pottery on the island.

QUADRUPEDS

The only quadrupeds indigenous to Jamaica are
the coney or agouti, with bats and a few wild rats
and mice. Manatees are common on the coast.

RAILWAYS

Tourist tickets good on all lines (first class only)
are issued at £4 ($20.00) each. These may be ob-
tained at any railway station or from the Tourist
Bureau, 87 Barry Street, Kingston, or from the
larger hotels. Such tourist tickets are good for one
calendar month, by all regular trains, over all lines
of the government railway, between any stations,
and in any direction.

The Jamaica Government Railway operates 210
miles of lines, and where tourist centers or towns
with accommodations for tourists are not on the
railway, coaches, busses or cars meet all trains.

In most cases round-trip tickets, called return
fares in Jamaica, are sold at considerably less
than two full trips. Thus the return fare to Williamsfield Station (Mandeville) is 15s. 9d., while
the one way ticket costs 10s. 6d.

The round-trip rate between Kingston and
Montego Bay is £1-14s-6d: Between Port Antonio

and Kingston, £1-2s-9d: Moneague and Kingston, 8s-3d.

(Baggage Charges)

No charge is made for transferring baggage from steamships to customs examination rooms.

Hotel porters meet all ships and attend to transfer of baggage for guests of their hotels, the charges for baggage, if any, being added to the hotel bill. The legal charge for handling baggage from customs to cart, dray or lorry, and delivery to any point in Kingston is 1s. (25¢) per piece, irrespective of size; but it is customary to pay a minimum charge of 2s.-6d. (60¢.)

(Porters)

Hotel porters are not entitled to any fees. Independent porters who accompany visitors and help them to secure accommodations and attend to luggage should be paid about 3s (75¢) for their services. Always arrange as to charges and fees in advance, to prevent being overcharged by porters, truckmen or others.

Rules of the Road

In Jamaica, the English rules of traffic hold good—Keep to the left and overtake on the right.

Religion

Although the Church of England is of course the dominant religion in Jamaica, there are no restrictions as to religious faiths or services. There are many churches—as well as schools—of the Baptists, Wesleyans, Presbyterians, Christian Scientists, Friends (Quakers), Seventh Day Adventists, Moravians, Methodists, Roman Catholics, etc. Many of the Portuguese inhabitants and others are of the Jewish faith. The Church of England Cathedral at Spanish Town is the oldest cathedral in the British colonies. The Roman Catholic Cathedral of the Holy Trinity is in Kingston. Altogether there are more than one thousand churches, chapels and missions on the island.

SCULPTURE

There are many monuments, statues and other works of sculpture in Jamaica, and of the more noted twelve examples of eighteenth century sculpture ten are from the famous Bacon. The two other are an Ionic monument in Halfway Tree Church by John Cheere, which is in honor of James Lawes, a son of Sir Nicholas Lawes, a former governor; and a monument to Lieutenant Stapleton in Port Royal Church, made by Roubiliac. Of Bacon's work the most noted is the Rodney Memorial in Spanish Town of which mention already has been made (Chapter III), the Effingham Monument in the English Cathedral and the Rose Palmer Monument in the church at Montego Bay.

Other notable sculptures are the monument to Lady Elgin, by Sir John Steell, in the cathedral;

the monument to Sir Charles Metcalfe, by Baily, in King Street, Kingston; the bust of the Rev. John Radcliffe, by Sir Thomas Brock, in the Scotch Church in Kingston; and the Archbishop Nuttall monument, by Albert Toft, in the cathedral.

SHOOTING (See Sports)

SNAKES AND LIZARDS

There are few tropical lands where snakes are as rare as in Jamaica. No poisonous snakes occur, and the few harmless species have been practically exterminated by the mongoose. Five species are known, and all are now very rare. The largest species is the Jamaican boa, a small species of the boa family very similar to the maja snake of Cuba, and perfectly harmless. All of the lizards are harmless, and the largest, the iguana, is extinct on the main island although still common on some of the outlying cays and small islets offshore.

SPORTS

Wherever there are British there is always an abundance of outdoor sports, and Jamaica is no exception to the rule. Every outdoor sport is featured on the island, and visitors can enjoy their favorite recreation be it golf, tennis, cricket, football, fishing, shooting, polo or anything aside from baseball.

HORSE RACING, the foremost of all English sports,

is very popular in Jamacia and has been ever since the island's occupation by the British. Although to a judge of the "ponies" the rather weedy-looking Jamaican horses are far from promising in appearance, yet many of them are near-thoroughbreds, and the finest equine blood of the English turf runs in their veins. In addition to the native horses entered in the races, a number are usually imported, while there are several stud farms on the island where thoroughbreds are raised.

The Kingston Racing Association holds meetings at Knutsford Park near Kingston. There are also races at Marlie (Old Harbour) and there are less important races held at Drax Hall, St. Ann, at Red Hills in St. Thomas, at Knollys in St. Catherine and at Cape Valley in Trelawny.

POLO matches are also held frequently. Before the Great War there were seven polo clubs in Jamaica, but during the war no polo was played and the game never has regained its former status. Under the auspices of the All Jamaica Polo Association the game is played at Up-Park Camp and at St. Ann. A junior and a senior cup are competed for twice each year.

CRICKET. "The grand old game" is a prime favorite with the colored population, as well as with the resident British, and from time to time teams come from England to compete with the local teams. In return, the West Indian teams go to England to play matches, and in each instance

Jamaicans have been members of these teams. There are cricket clubs in every parish and town, just as we have our village baseball nines.

In Kingston there are several good matches yearly, the most important being the Senior Cup Competition. There are also the Minor, Junior and Sunlight Competitions for schoolboys.

LAWN TENNIS. This is probably the most popular out-of-doors game in the British West Indies. For many years an annual match has been held for a challenge cup. In Jamaica the leading clubs have organized the Jamaica Law Tennis Association, affiliated with the Law Tennis Association of England, and have arranged a yearly match for two challenge cups. Interclub matches are open to certain visitors to the island. There is a hard-court competition at Mandeville once a year.

GOLF. Although golf has been played in Jamaica for more than thirty years it cannot be said to be a very popular game among the residents. In fact, from the very beginning, it has been mainly dependent upon visitors from overseas. Largely owing to lack of funds, no really good independent club with its own links and club-houses has been established and while there are various small golf clubs on the island they are usually branches of country clubs or are maintained by the hotels for the benefit of guests. There is a nine hole course at the Liguanea Club, three miles from Kingston, and another nine hole course at Robin's Bay. The St.

Mary's Country Club also has a nine hole course. Small courses are at Mandeville and at Moneague and at Montego Bay there is a six hole course.

FOOTBALL. Football, or as we call it, "Soccer," is very popular in Jamaica, and the black and colored boys are seen playing the game everywhere. The real football season is from October until February. There are several organized clubs, both civilian and military, and the Jamaica Association Football Challenge Shield has been competed for each year since 1898. The Martinez Cup is for civilian teams only, while the Manning Cup is for secondary school teams of Kingston and the Olivier Shield is open to all secondary school teams. In Jamaica the time of play is forty minutes instead of sixty as in temperate climates.

HOCKEY is played only at some of the girls' schools.

CROQUET, in its scientific form, has become quite popular of recent years.

RIFLE SHOOTING. Rifle clubs exist among the militia, the police and civilians, and rifle shooting is being introduced into the Jamaican schools.

The Swettenham Rifle Cup, presented for competition among West Indian teams, has often been won, and is at present held, by the Jamaican marksmen. There is a Jamaica Schools Miniature Rifle Association and the Perkins Shield is annually competed for.

YACHTING. The Royal Jamaica Yacht Club has

its headquarters at Kingston and holds an annual regatta, usually at the time of the visit of the British Fleet.

SEA BATHING. Bathing is very popular and is possible in nearly all portions of Jamaica. Unfortunately there is no really good beach near Kingston, but the Bournemouth Baths are quite satisfactory. At various resorts near Port Antonio, at Montego Bay, Doctor's Cave, Dunn's River, St. Ann's, and practically everywhere else on the island, the bathing is excellent. The water is as clear as glass and remains at an even temperature of 80° F.

SHOOTING. Although there is no big game in Jamaica, and no game animals of any description, there is excellent game bird shooting to be had in the season. The principal game hunted in Jamaica are the wild pigeons of several varieties, such as the blue pigeon, bald-pate, ring-tail, white-wing, pea-dove, white-belly and partridge. In addition to these there are numbers of migratory ducks, teal, snipe, plover and other water-fowl. In Jamaica the butter bird or ortolan—our own bob-o-link—is considered a game bird. Broadly speaking, the Jamaican shooting season is from August to October, although it extends until March, the length of season depending very largely upon the rains. In a dry season there is excellent pigeon shooting until the end of November, whereas in rainy weather the birds stop flying and remain in the mountain forests, while the reverse is the case with duck and snipe. The latter furnish the best sport on the island. The favorite snipe grounds are old cane fields, the open pastures or commons, and woodlands that are soggy from rains. At the end of the season, from February to March, there is the guinea-corn shooting when the pigeons flock to the corn and afford excellent sport, for the Jamaican wild pigeons are by no means easy marks. This is especially true of the white-winged pigeon which has a habit of closing its wings when several hundred yards from its feeding ground and fairly hurtling down like a feathered bullet. The small size of the bird when thus plunging down and the speed with which it travels makes it, in the estimation of many, the most difficult mark of all game birds.

FISHING. Jamaica is famous for the great variety of fishes with which the waters teem. Many are splendid game fish, and the angler will find plenty of sport in Jamaican waters. In the rivers and estuaries the principal game fish are the tarpon, snook, snapper and jack. Mountain mullet are found in most of the rivers. The Black River, especially, is a noted fishing ground. Tarpon weighing as much as one hundred pounds, snappers weighing over one hundred pounds, enormous groupers; jacks up to twenty-five pounds, and snooks weighing fifteen pounds are not unusual. Among the commonest sea fish taken are king fish, Spanish mackerel, barracuda, cavally, bonito, etc.

[228]

Montego Bay is one of the best spots for sea fishing. In regard to tackle and bait it is best to consult the local fishermen. Finally, for those who want more exciting sport, there are sharks and crocodiles (miscalled alligators) which are very abundant.

TAXI-CABS

Taxi-cabs are distinguished by having a white band two inches in width around the body of the car. The legal fares from Victoria Pier, King Street and neighboring points to the principal places in the surrounding district are as follows:

From 6 A. M. until 10 P. M.

		per person
To	Matilda's Corner	3s. 6d.
”	Trafalgar Park	2s. 6d.
”	King's House Gate	2s. 6d.
”	Halfway Tree	2s. 6d.
”	Liguanea Club and Golf Course	2s.
”	Up-Park Camp	2s.
”	Bournemouth Bath	1s. 6d.
”	Cross Roads	1s. 6d.
”	Movies Picture House, Cross Roads	1s. 6d.
”	St. Andrew's Club	1s. 6d.
”	St. George's Club	6d.
”	Melbourne and Clovelly Cricket Clubs	6d.
”	Railway Station	6d.
”	Jamaica Club	6d.

  " Palace Picture House   6d.
  " Gaiety Picture House   6d.
  " Y. M. C. A., Hanover Street   6d.

	Taxis	Carriages
By time, between 6 A. M. and 10 P. M., for half an hour or less	4s.	2s.
For any length of time exceeding one half hour and not exceeding one hour	10s.	5s.
For every additional half hour or part thereof after the first hour	4s.	2s.

Between 10 P. M. and 6 A. M. the rates are double the above.

These rates apply only to the Corporate areas of Kingston and St. Andrew.

If taking a carriage or taxi outside these areas a bargain should be made in advance.

TENNIS (See Sports)

TREES

In Jamaica there are few deciduous trees, as we know them. Nearly all the trees are evergreens, in that they are constantly shedding their leaves and producing new ones coincidently. And when deciduous trees, do occur—as the ceibas or silk-cotton trees—they stand out like sore fingers, stark and naked. Many of the largest forest trees bear magnificent and gorgeous flowers, for in the tropics many of the trees belong to the violet, verbena, heliotrope or similar families and bloom in much the same manner as their herbaceous relatives. The lignum-vitæ has masses of pale-blue or white flowers. The mountain pride seems like a solid pyramid of rose-purple blooms. The Spanish elm is a mass of snow-white when in flower. The coratoes exhibit great candelabra-shaped masses of yellow of various shades. The flowers of the West Indian ebony are brilliant yellow and have the effect of bursting into bloom after every shower. The bastard cabbage-bark tree drapes its limbs with clusters of lavender flowers like wisteria blossoms, and of course there are the acacias and the mimosas, together with the various poincianas with their flowers of innumerable shades of scarlet and crimson. Of palms there are about a dozen native species known, while many others, such as the coconut palms, the wax palms, the ivory-nut palms, the talipot palms, the royal palms, etc., are introduced species.

WATER SUPPLY

The supply of drinking water in Kingston is of the highest quality and may be used with perfect confidence. It is obtained from several sources; from Hope River, Wag Water, Ferry River and the Hermitage Dam, and is thoroughly purified and filtered. Even the smaller towns have excellent water supplies and these constantly are being improved.

YACHTING (See Sports)